STAND
on the
WORD
Study Guide

1 SAMUEL

LONGING FOR A KING

A 14-Day Journey through the Word

with Tony Perkins

FIDELIS PUBLISHING ®

ISBN: 9798994581346

1 Samuel: Longing for a King
A 14–Day Journey through the Book of 1 Samuel
A Stand on the Word Study Guide

Content contributor: Dr. Kenyn Cureton
Cover design: Diana Lawrence
Copyediting and interior typesetting: Lisa Parnell

Order at www.faithfultext.com for a significant discount. Email info@fidelispublishing.com to inquire about bulk purchase discounts.

Fidelis Publishing, LLC Winchester, VA • Nashville, TN www.fidelispublishing.com

Manufactured in the United States of America

10 9 8 7 6 5 4 3 2 1

FIDELIS PUBLISHING

Contents

1 Samuel: An Introduction

Welcome to the Stand on the Word Study Guide *1 Samuel: Longing for a King*. This book, as well as its sequel, is named for Samuel because it begins with his story, as he is the last judge of Israel. In fact, Samuel fills multiple roles. He functions as a judge, a priest, and a prophet, and in that sense, he is a type of Christ. Three principal figures dominate the storyline of this amazing book: Samuel, Saul, and David. Samuel functions as sort of a bridge from the period of the Judges to the period of the Kings. Consequently, God is transitioning the nation to a different form of government in response to their longing for a king.

Yet through the books of 1–2 Samuel, 1–2 Kings, and 1–2 Chronicles, we find that the form of government, while it is significant, is not the determining factor of the prosperity and well-being of the people and a nation's success. The determining factor is whether the nation chooses to fear and follow God or not, which shapes the character of a people. That determines the success of a nation: the godly character of the people and particularly of the leaders.

As to the author of this book, tradition holds that Samuel wrote chapters 1–25. Then according to 1 Chronicles 29:29, Nathan and Gad finished the books. As to the date of its writing, it was completed between 1050 to 1000 BC. The overall message of 1 Samuel is one of revival. This book calls the people back to the true worship of God. Though the people long for a king like the rest of the nations, we are reminded that Yahweh is the divine King of Israel.

The outline of the book is simple, following the three major characters in the book:

1. The Rise of Samuel: God Restores Spiritual Leadership (chaps. 1–7)
2. The Reign of Saul: Man's Choice for a King (chaps. 8–15)
3. The Rise of David: God's Choice for a King (chaps. 16–31)

Each of these characters—Samuel, Saul, and David—reveal something vital about leadership and the heart. Samuel demonstrates what it means to live a life surrendered to God's voice. Saul, though impressive in appearance and initially successful, becomes a sobering example of what happens when outward position is not matched by inward submission. David, though far from perfect, shows us that God delights in a heart that passionately pursues Him.

Throughout 1 Samuel, a consistent truth rises to the surface: The condition of the heart determines the direction of the life. This was true for Israel, and it remains true for us today. In a world that often values appearance over character and success over obedience, this book calls us back to what truly matters. It challenges us to consider who or what we are trusting, and whether our hearts are fully aligned with God's Word.

As we begin this study, come with a humble and receptive spirit. Allow the Word of God to search your heart and shape your life. Like the young Samuel, may this become your prayer as you open each day's reading: "Speak, LORD, for Your servant hears." And may your time in 1 Samuel lead not only to greater understanding but to a deeper surrender to the Lord who alone is worthy to reign as King.

How to Get the Most from the Study Guide

While the study guide offers spiritual insights and applications, the real impact comes from the words of Scripture, which is the Word of God. Please read the selected text for the day in your own Bible. God's Word is living and active (Heb. 4:12). The Spirit of God uses His Word to change your life. Nothing else can do that. So before reading the daily commentary, read God's Word! In fact, here are five habits to cultivate as you approach God's Word each day.

1. *Read it through:* Do not skip around. Read the entire selection of Scripture. If you are pressed for time, please read the Bible before you read the study guide notes. So read it through.
2. *Think it over:* Meditate on it. Let it marinate in your mind. If you can, take notes. We provide a notes page at the end of each day. Think it over.
3. *Pray it in:* Personalize the Scripture. Turn the verse that speaks to you into a prayer, and then pray it into your life. Ask God what you need to do in response. This leads to the next habit.
4. *Live it out:* Consider ways to apply what God is revealing to you, ways you can obey Him. Put His Word into practice. Make it a part of who you are, how you think, how you speak, and behave toward God and other people. In other words, take God's Word and live it out.
5. *Pass it on.* Do not keep it to yourself. There are people in your life who need the same truth God has spoken to you in His Word. Share it. Pass it on.

About Stand on the Word

Stand on the Word is a ministry of Family Research Council, whose mission is to serve in the kingdom of God by championing faith, family, and freedom in public policy and the culture from a biblical worldview. The purpose of Stand on the Word is to lay the foundation for a biblical worldview through daily reading and application of God's Word. For the daily journey, we have created a chronologically prioritized reading plan through the entire Bible that can be accessed at frc.org/Bible or simply by texting the word *Bible* to 67742.

Land Unconquered by the End of Saul's Reign

— Day 1 —

Today's Reading: 1 Samuel 1–2

Verse of the Day

> And the child Samuel grew in stature, and in favor both with the LORD and men.
>
> — *1 Samuel 2:26*

Please read the entire Scripture selection in your own Bible and highlight or underline verses that stand out to you before you read the observations and engage the questions below.

Today we begin chapters 1–2 in our study of 1 Samuel. Our key verse is 1 Samuel 2:26, "And the child Samuel grew in stature, and in favor both with the LORD and men." Samuel is one of the purest servants of the Lord in terms of heart and focus whom we read about in the Scripture. Chapter 1 offers a brief background of Samuel, with the focus on his mother, Hannah, who was barren and one of the two wives of Elkanah. Here we are reminded of the pivotal role that women play in the history of the nation of Israel and, by extension, the Christian faith. In these two chapters, we see the power of a praying mother contrasted with the powerful position of a passive father, and in the end, we discover that the praying mother has the greatest influence.

We read about her desperate prayer in 1 Samuel 1:9–14:

> So Hannah arose after they had finished eating and drinking in Shiloh. Now Eli the priest was sitting on the seat by the

> doorpost of the tabernacle of the LORD. And she was in bitterness of soul, and prayed to the LORD and wept in anguish. Then she made a vow and said, "O LORD of hosts, if You will indeed look on the affliction of Your maidservant and remember me, and not forget Your maidservant, but will give Your maidservant a male child, then I will give him to the LORD all the days of his life, and no razor shall come upon his head." And it happened, as she continued praying before the LORD, that Eli watched her mouth. Now Hannah spoke in her heart; only her lips moved, but her voice was not heard. Therefore Eli thought she was drunk. So Eli said to her, "How long will you be drunk? Put your wine away from you!"

Obviously, Eli misread what was happening with Hannah. Unfortunately, this speaks both to the poor spiritual conditions of the culture at the time and Eli's cynical outlook. He probably saw something similar with his own sons, who we read about in the next chapter as being corrupt and not knowing the Lord. Look at verses 15–17: "But Hannah answered and said, 'No, my lord, I am a woman of sorrowful spirit. I have drunk neither wine nor intoxicating drink, but have poured out my soul before the LORD. Do not consider your maidservant a wicked woman, for out of the abundance of my complaint and grief I have spoken until now.' Then Eli answered and said, 'Go in peace, and the God of Israel grant your petition which you have asked of Him.'" This episode reminds me of Matthew 18:19, which speaks to the power of agreement in prayer: "'Again I say to you that if two of you agree on earth concerning anything that they ask, it will be done for them by My Father in heaven.'"

As the narrative progresses, God answers and Hannah had a son. When young Samuel was weaned, which was probably around the age of three, his parents took him to the tabernacle to serve the Lord and left him there. Continue in 1 Samuel 2:11–12: "Then Elkanah went to his house at Ramah. But the child ministered to the LORD before Eli the priest. Now the sons of Eli were corrupt; they did not know the LORD." Note here that the root of corruption is not knowing the Lord. It is also worth noting the stark contrast made between young Samuel and Eli's corrupt sons. For example, we read in verse 18, "But Samuel ministered before the LORD, even as a child, wearing a linen ephod." Truly, Samuel was a better son to Eli than his own.

Yet not only do we see the contrast between Eli's sons and Samuel, but we also see the contrast between Hannah, the praying mother, and Eli, the passive father. Continue in verse 19: "Moreover his mother used to make him a little robe, and bring it to him year by year when she came up with her husband to offer the yearly sacrifice." While the Scripture does not tell us this explicitly, based on what we know of Hannah, it is likely that she prayed regularly for Samuel, and she thought of him in his service before the Lord continually. This stands in sharp contrast to Eli, as we read in 1 Samuel 2:22–23: "Now Eli was very old; and he heard everything his sons did to all Israel, and how they lay with the women who assembled at the door of the tabernacle of meeting. So he said to them, 'Why do you do such things? For I hear of your evil dealings from all the people.'" So, his sons were having sexual relations with the women as they came to the tabernacle.

However, the sin was not limited to Eli's sons as we read further in verses 24–26: "'No, my sons! For it is not a good report that I hear. You make the LORD's people transgress. If one man sins against another, God will judge him. But if a man sins against the LORD, who will intercede for him?' Nevertheless they did not heed the voice of their father, because the Lord desired to kill them. And the child Samuel grew in stature, and in favor both with the LORD and men." Sound familiar? It was said of Jesus in Luke 2:52, "And Jesus increased in wisdom and stature, and in favor with God and men." God had his hand of favor on young Samuel, while His hand of judgment was about to fall on Eli's sons. What a stark contrast!

What did Eli do? Other than plead with his sons and say, "Do not do this," he did not do anything. He did not remove them from their duties. Further, the Bible says these two derelicts despised the offerings of the Lord, treating the holy things of God with contempt. This sad story sounds similar to that of Nadab and Abihu in Leviticus 10 where their contempt of the holy things of God cost them their very lives. They were consumed by the fire of the Lord. Question: Did Eli's sons know what happened to Nadab and Abihu? Did they know their history? The nation's history? This is why history is important because you know God is the same yesterday, today, and forever.

Now, Eli's indifference, a father refusing to correct the behavior of his sons, brought judgment from God. And as we are going to see here, it was not only judgment upon the two sons but upon the family and the nation. We read this of the man of God in 1 Samuel 2:27–30:

> Then a man of God came to Eli and said to him, "Thus says the LORD: 'Did I not clearly reveal Myself to the house of your father when they were in Egypt in Pharaoh's house? Did I not choose him out of all the tribes of Israel to be My priest, to offer upon My altar, to burn incense, and to wear an ephod before Me? And did I not give to the house of your father all the offerings of the children of Israel made by fire? Why do you kick at My sacrifice and My offering which I have commanded in My dwelling place, and honor your sons more than Me, to make yourselves fat with the best of all the offerings of Israel My people?' Therefore the LORD God of Israel says: 'I said indeed that your house and the house of your father would walk before Me forever.' But now the LORD says: 'Far be it from Me; for those who honor Me I will honor, and those who despise Me shall be lightly esteemed.'"

Please do not miss this point: Eli was the high priest of the nation, but he failed to be the spiritual leader of his home. From what we read here, Eli knew his sons were doing wrong. Yet Eli showed more deference to his sons than honor toward God. He was more concerned about what his sons thought than what God did. He was more afraid to offend his sons than he feared offending God. We see this today. We are afraid to lose the affections of our children, afraid to offend them because we want to be their friends rather than be their parents, as God has called us. The result is that we both offend God and we lose our children—not a winning proposition.

Hannah put God first. She prayed for her son and gave him to the Lord. By contrast, we see no mention of Eli praying for his sons nor giving them to the Lord. Rather, it suggested he held on to them, placing a higher priority on trying to please them than please God. Whose example should we choose to follow? That of Hannah or of Eli? The passive posture of Eli toward his sons' behavior, which dishonored God, resulted in his family being removed from the exalted position of the priesthood, and it also adversely affected the nation.

Consider what God prophetically declares in 1 Samuel 2:31: "'Behold, the days are coming that I will cut off your arm and the arm of your father's house, so that there will not be an old man in your house.'" God holds us accountable for our stewardship as spiritual leaders. We must especially address sin in our own homes. Sin has grave consequences, and we must lovingly confront it.

In these chapters, we see Hannah, a mother who took her spiritual stewardship as a parent seriously. She was a praying woman and ultimately had an incredibly positive impact on the nation through offering her son to the Lord. At the same time, we see the stark contrast with Eli, who was a passive father and refused to confront the sin of his sons. His failure will become even more evident as the story unfolds.

Prayer

Father, thank You for Your Word. What a wonderful story of Hannah, a mother who literally helped shape a nation through her prayer and dedication to You. And Lord, we see this passive father who had a title and had a position. Yet Eli chose his sons over You, not wanting to confront their sin. Lord, we pray that You will give us all praying hearts that are passionate for You. May we not take Your Word and ways lightly, but, Lord, that we will put You first and seek to please You in all that we do, beginning in our homes and in our relationships. This we pray in Jesus's name. Amen.

Questions for Reflection and Discussion

1. What do Hannah's prayers tell us about how she understood God (see 2:1–10)?

2. What did Eli do about his sons' sinful behavior as priests, and how did they respond (see 2:25)?

Notes on Today's Bible Reading

— Day 2 —

Today's Reading: 1 Samuel 3–4

Verse of the Day

> Now the boy Samuel ministered to the Lord before Eli. And the word of the Lord was rare in those days; there was no widespread revelation.
>
> — *1 Samuel 3:1*

Please read the entire Scripture selection in your own Bible and highlight or underline verses that stand out to you before you read the observations and engage the questions below.

Today, we are in 1 Samuel 3–4. Our key verse is 1 Samuel 3:1: "Now the boy Samuel ministered to the Lord before Eli. And the word of the Lord was rare in those days; there was no widespread revelation." This first verse describes the poor spiritual condition of the nation. The meaning of the word *revelation* here means communication or actions of the Lord were rare. They did not hear from, communicate with, or see God moving. Consequently, this was a spiritually barren time. The question is, Why did God just choose to stop communicating with His people? Well, we explore that question as we look into the chapters in today's reading.

Look at 1 Samuel 3:2–5: "And it came to pass at that time, while Eli was lying down in his place, and when his eyes had begun to grow so dim that he could not see, and before the lamp of God went out in the tabernacle of the Lord where the ark of God was, and while Samuel was lying down, that the LORD called Samuel. And he answered, 'Here I am!' So he ran to Eli and said, 'Here I am, for you called me.' And he said, 'I did not call; lie down again.' And he went and lay down." Note that it was Samuel who was primarily serving Eli, not Eli's sons. Most likely, Samuel had become very dear to Eli as it became increasingly evident that God's hand was upon this young man (see 2:26).

Next, we read in 1 Samuel 3:6–7: "Then the LORD called yet again, 'Samuel!' So Samuel arose and went to Eli, and said, 'Here I am, for you called me.' He answered, 'I did not call, my son; lie down again.' (Now Samuel did not yet know the LORD, nor was the word of the LORD yet revealed to him.)" For context, this biblical account is the focus of popular stories for children. In those stories, Samuel is always seen as a small child, and the Hebrew word *na'ar* translated as "boy" back in verse 1 can certainly mean that. In fact, the Greek Septuagint version has *paidarion*, which is translated "little boy" or "lad," the same word used in the New Testament of the boy with the loaves and fishes (see John 6:9).

Yet, the Hebrew word can also refer to a male who is an adolescent. In fact, the Jewish historian, Josephus, took Samuel to be twelve years old at this time.[1] However, the Hebrew word is so broad in its application, it can even mean a young man up to around twenty years of age. Interestingly, the age of accountability in Hebrew culture was twenty years old, which was the age of those who were to pay the half-shekel atonement offering to the Lord (Exod. 30:14) as well as counted in the census for military service (Num. 1:3). Furthermore, apprenticeship for service as a priest began at age twenty (see 1 Chron. 23:24–27), and service in the sanctuary began at twenty-five (Num. 8:24–25). Modern research shows that our brains are not fully developed until our mid-twenties. This is historically why we have not allowed adolescents to make certain life altering decisions. Of course, that is changing for political reasons. But back to the point: The popular interpretation is that Samuel was a young boy, but it is possible that Samuel was around twenty years old when God called him. Regardless of his age, what is even more important is that God called him to become more than a priest, as we see in the verses that follow.

Continue in 1 Samuel 3:8: “And the LORD called Samuel again the third time. So he arose and went to Eli, and said, ‘Here I am, for you did call me.’” Eli, the high priest, recognized that God was calling Samuel, so he told the young man what to do. Then we read in verses 9–10, “Therefore Eli said to Samuel, ‘Go, lie down; and it shall be, if He calls you, that you must say, “Speak, LORD, for Your servant hears.”’ So Samuel went and lay down in his place. Now the LORD came and stood and called as at other times, ‘Samuel! Samuel!’ And Samuel answered, ‘Speak, for Your servant hears.’”

Here are three things to consider by way of application. First, God still speaks. In a day when the word of God was rarely heard, Samuel heard God speak. The Lord was preparing to break through all the spiritual darkness with fresh revelation. Even in seasons when truth seems scarce and compromise abounds, God is still speaking. Today, He speaks through His Word, the Bible. Second, God calls us personally. He called Samuel by name. The repetition is tender and relational. Scripture shows time and again that God’s calling is personal. Third, listening requires humility: “Speak, for your servant hears.” Again, the question is not whether God is speaking but whether we are listening. The posture of listening is that of a servant who is surrendered.

Next comes the message from the Lord in 3:11–14:

> Then the LORD said to Samuel: “Behold, I will do something in Israel at which both ears of everyone who hears it will tingle. In that day I will perform against Eli all that I have spoken concerning his house, from beginning to end. For I have told him that I will judge his house forever for the iniquity which he knows, because his sons made themselves vile, and he did

> not restrain them. And therefore I have sworn to the house of Eli that the iniquity of Eli's house shall not be atoned for by sacrifice or offering forever."

Eli had been warned, yet he allowed his sons to continue in their sins without restraint and did not correct them. His sin was willful. Though Eli and his sons held sacred office, served at the tabernacle, and handled holy things, their spiritual privilege did not exempt them from God's judgment.

Then we read in 1 Samuel 3:15–17, "So Samuel lay down until morning, and opened the doors of the house of the Lord. And Samuel was afraid to tell Eli the vision. Then Eli called Samuel and said, 'Samuel, my son!' He answered, 'Here I am.' And he said, 'What is the word that the Lord spoke to you? Please do not hide it from me. God do so to you, and more also, if you hide anything from me of all the things that He said to you.'" Pause there for just a moment. This is why God had stopped speaking to Eli. The spiritual leader had not been listening. You see, if we fail or refuse to act upon the word that the Lord has given us, we should not expect God to keep communicating. In fact, refusing to listen will result in the inability to hear. The Lord wanted to communicate with His people. So, since Eli wouldn't listen, God spoke to Samuel instead.

With this message from the Lord came Samuel's first test. Would he honor and follow the Lord whom he had just personally encountered, or would he yield to the same human desire for acceptance that Eli did with his sons? Well, that was the downfall of Eli. He wanted the acceptance of those around him more than he wanted to please and obey God. Think about the fact that Eli was like a father to Samuel. Yet Samuel had a message from God telling Eli that it was over. He had sinned and God was about to bring judgment upon his house.

Here is the question: In this first test of allegiance, would Samuel follow God, or would he try to please Eli? Look at 1 Samuel

3:18–21: "Then Samuel told him everything, and hid nothing from him. And he said, 'It is the LORD. Let Him do what seems good to Him.' So Samuel grew, and the LORD was with him and let none of his words fall to the ground. And all Israel from Dan to Beersheba knew that Samuel had been established as a prophet of the LORD. Then the LORD appeared again in Shiloh. For the LORD revealed Himself to Samuel in Shiloh by the word of the LORD." The result was that Samuel honored God in this first test. Therefore God then honored Samuel, and the people were the beneficiaries.

Compare the first verse of chapter 3 with this last verse. We read in 1 Samuel 3:1b, "And the word of the LORD was rare in those days; there was no widespread revelation." Yet then we read in 1 Samuel 3:21, "Then the LORD appeared again in Shiloh. For the LORD revealed Himself to Samuel in Shiloh by the word of the LORD." Why the difference? Because the young man listened and obeyed. You see, we have to obey the Word of God if we want to continue to see God moving in our midst. There is nothing that will stifle the move of God more than disobedience.

One of my favorite places to visit in Israel is Shiloh. This is the location where this episode in 1 Samuel unfolded. Shiloh was the place of the tabernacle for 369 years. People came from all over Israel to bring their offerings to the Lord and to worship Him. It was the place of His presence. What captivates me about Shiloh is the fact that you can actually see the stone perimeter, the outline of what is said to have been where the tabernacle stood for nearly four centuries. You can also see hundreds of thousands of pottery shards all over the ground from the earthen vessels that were broken after the offerings were made to the Lord. Yet this place, filled with spiritual significance, came to a tragic end when the glory of the Lord departed from the nation. When I stand on that spot, which really was the center of Jewish identity, the source of their strength for nearly four hundred years, and then read this account of Eli, I cannot help but be gripped by the sobering reality that Eli, even though he had the title of high priest, failed as a father to be the spiritual leader of his home. The result was both personal and national tragedy.

In chapter 4, we see God begin to fulfill the message that He delivered to Samuel. When they went out to battle against the Philistines, Eli's sons took the ark of the covenant, which represented the presence of God. Yet for them, the ark merely represented a good-luck charm. But their "luck" ran out. Though the ark was with them, the presence of God was not. They were defeated by the Philistines, and the ark was captured. Word came back to Eli that Israel was defeated, the ark was captured, and the sons were dead. He fell off his stool, broke his neck, and he died.

When Eli's distressed daughter-in-law who was with child heard the news, she went into premature labor. We read of the tragic result in 1 Samuel 4:20–22: "And about the time of her death the women who stood by her said to her, 'Do not fear, for you have borne a son.' But she did not answer, nor did she regard it. Then she named the child Ichabod, saying, 'The glory has departed from Israel!' because the ark of God had been captured and because of her father-in-law and her husband. And she said, 'The glory has departed from Israel, for the ark of God has been captured.'" Tragically, the name "Ichabod" was a prophetic description of Israel at this low point.

As we complete today's study, here is the takeaway: Compromise in the home leads to corruption in the culture, and it has consequences for an entire nation. Eli did not restrain his sons. As we read in chapter 2, he honored them or preferred them more than God. Question: Do parents do that today? Unfortunately, they do. The results may not be as dramatic as we read here. Regardless, it does not end well when we prefer our children over God. If we put anything before God, including our family members, that person or thing becomes an idol. And God says in Matthew 6:33, "But seek first the kingdom of God and His righteousness, and all these things shall be added to you." You know, all of these tragic results could have been avoided if Eli, the spiritual leader, had put God first by listening to and obeying Him.

Prayer

Father, thank You for Your Word, and, Lord, this is an amazing account of Eli and Samuel. And what a contrast: a young man who is willing to listen and obey compared to an older man who had the title, had the position, but he wouldn't obey; he no longer could hear the voice of the Lord giving direction, and the whole nation suffered as a result. Father, we pray that in our homes we hear, we listen, and we obey. And Lord, as we do that in our families, may our churches do it. And may we see that in communities. And may our nation once again respond in obedience to You. We pray and ask this in Jesus's name. Amen.

Questions for Reflection and Discussion

1. What did Eli coach young Samuel to say to God when He called (see 3:9)?
2. What does the story about the capture of the ark of the covenant teach us (see 4:1–11)? Is it possible to feel confident God is on our side when He is not?

Notes on Today's Bible Reading

— Day 3 —

Today's Reading: 1 Samuel 5–7

Verse of the Day

> Then Samuel spoke to all the house of Israel, saying, "If you return to the LORD with all your hearts, then put away the foreign gods and the Ashtoreths from among you, and prepare your hearts for the LORD, and serve Him only; and He will deliver you from the hand of the Philistines."
>
> *—1 Samuel 7:3*

Please read the entire Scripture selection in your own Bible and highlight or underline verses that stand out to you before you read the observations and engage the questions below.

We study 1 Samuel 5–7 today, which relates the aftermath of Israel's tragic defeat at the hands of the Philistines; the capture of the ark of the covenant but then followed by its return; and finally, the revival led by Samuel, which resulted in God giving Israel triumph over the enemy. Our key verse is 1 Samuel 7:3: "Then Samuel spoke to all the house of Israel, saying, 'If you return to the LORD with all your hearts, then put away the foreign gods and the Ashtoreths from among you, and prepare your hearts for the LORD, and serve Him only; and He will deliver you from the hand of the Philistines.'"

In chapter 5, the Philistines take the captured ark as a trophy of war to Ashdod. They placed it in the temple of their god, Dagon, who was their chief deity. That idol depicted a man-fish creature that personified their belief that the primeval waters were the source from which both men and fish had evolved. Additionally, Dagon was said to be the father of Baal, the supreme Canaanite deity, as well as being the provider of grain. Note what happens to Dagon in 1 Samuel 5:3: "And when the people of Ashdod arose early in the morning, there was Dagon, fallen on its face to the earth before the ark of the Lord. So they took Dagon and set it in its place again." Then we read in verse 4, "And when they arose early the next morning, there was Dagon, fallen on its face to the ground before the ark of the Lord. The head of Dagon and both the palms of its hands were broken off on the threshold; only Dagon's torso was left of it." In this satirical account, the statue of Dagon is discovered bowing before the ark. By showing the people trying to prop up a broken idol, Samuel is mocking the absurdity of idol worship.

However, then the story turns serious when we read that God afflicted the people of Ashdod with painful tumors and causing panic (see vv. 6–7). Note the stark contrast between the powerless hands of Dagon that had been broken off with the powerful hand of God that was heavy and harsh upon them. To escape the Lord's plague in Ashdod, the Philistine leaders decided in verse 8b, "'Let the ark of the God of Israel be carried away to Gath.'" Yet when they moved the ark to Gath, the same afflictions and a "very great destruction" from the hand of Yahweh followed it there. Consequently, the people of Gath sent the ark to Ekron. When it arrived there, the inhabitants cried out in terror, fearing for their lives, as we read in verse 10: "'They have brought the ark of the God of Israel to us, to kill us and our people!'" By the end of chapter 5, the Philistines suffered so much from the heavy hand of God, their leaders concluded that the ark must be returned to Israel in hopes of stopping the destruction (vv. 11–12).

Obviously, the Philistines were sorely mistaken about the one true God. They wrongly assumed the ark was just like one of their idols they could carry around, control, and use for their own purposes. Yet they found out that idols are much different than the one true and living God. Idols are gods we imagine who will yield to us and give us what we want based upon our unregenerated desires. That is what idols are.

We still see idol worship today, not only idols of stone, wood, or metal worshipped among primitive peoples not unlike the Philistines back in biblical times, but also the idols worshipped in more economically and technologically advanced cultures. Think of that smartphone everyone carries around that absorbs their time and attention. The average American spends more than five hours a day on their phone, checking it on average every five minutes, or two hundred times a day, scrolling through social media feeds, watching reels, and so on.[2] It has become an idol people carry around.

Yet we read that the God of Israel could not be controlled. Everywhere the ark went, a symbol of His presence, that territory may have been under the jurisdiction of the Philistines, but God overruled them all. As we read, God not only humbled their idols, but He also sent the plagues of rats and tumors. While the hands of their pagan god Dagon had been broken off, the hand of God could not be stayed. Chapter 5 highlights the fact that although Israel had been soundly defeated in battle, Yahweh God remains sovereign and undefeated.

In chapter 6, we continue the story with the Philistines trying to figure out how to get rid of the ark. After suffering for seven months, the Philistines consult their pagan priests and diviners. They are advised in verse 3, and the Philistine religious leaders suggested in verse 4 that they include a guilt offering of five golden tumors and five golden rats to appease Israel's God, adding this admonition in verses 5–6: "'Therefore you shall make images of your tumors and images of your rats that ravage the land, and you shall give glory to the God of Israel; perhaps He will lighten His hand from you, from your gods, and from your land. Why then do you harden your hearts as the Egyptians and Pharaoh hardened their hearts? When He did mighty things among them, did they not let the people go, that they might depart?'" Is that not amazing? They are counseling how the Philistines might "give glory to the God of Israel," even recalling His mighty acts in delivering Israel from Egypt and urging them not to harden their hearts. It almost sounds like an evangelistic invitation!

Yet there were some reservations about the cause of all the suffering, so they came up with a test in verses 7–12 to prove whether the God of Israel had judged them or the plagues were just simply the result of "chance." The Philistines were to place the ark of Yahweh on a new cart pulled by two milk cows that had never been yoked and had nursing calves. If the cows left their calves and headed straight for Israelite territory, it would be a miraculous sign of God's hand. This is an interesting revelation of the mindset of fallen man, of the world's view of God. We read further in verses 13–18 that the cows indeed headed directly to Beth Shemesh in Israel without turning aside and the Philistines got their answer and went back home.

When the ark arrived, we read in verse 13, "Now the people of Beth Shemesh were reaping their wheat harvest in the valley; and they lifted their eyes and saw the ark, and rejoiced to see it." Consequently, the Israelites offered the cows as a burnt offering to the Lord on a large stone in the field of Joshua the Beth Shemeshite. However, joy turned to terror when God struck a large number of men for daring to look inside the ark, prompting them to cry out in verse 20, "'Who is able to stand before this holy LORD God? And to whom shall it go up from us?'" The chapter ends with verse 21: "So they sent messengers to the inhabitants of Kirjath Jearim, saying, 'The Philistines have brought back the ark of the LORD; come down and take it up with you.'"

After reading two chapters of severe judgment, first on the Philistines and then on the Israelites, some might get the idea that

God somehow takes satisfaction in it. Yet God does not celebrate in or rejoice in judgment. His desire is actually for repentance. Ezekiel 18:23 says, "'Do I have any pleasure at all that the wicked should die?' says the Lord God, 'and not that he should turn from his ways and live?'" The Philistines created rats and tumors of gold as if somehow God would be appeased by it. That is not what God wants. God wants a repentant heart, a broken heart. God will not reject, but He will show mercy. In fact, James 2:13 declares, "Mercy triumphs over judgment." That is God's heart: Mercy over judgment. Will judgment come? Yes, if we disrespect His holiness and refuse to turn and repent. But God's mercy flows to our repentance. That is actually where we pick up in chapter 7, after the ark actually makes its way back to Israel on this cart pulled by cows.

Let us start in 1 Samuel 7:2–3: "So it was that the ark remained in Kirjath Jearim a long time; it was there twenty years. And all the house of Israel lamented after the Lord. Then Samuel spoke to all the house of Israel, saying, 'If you return to the Lord with all your hearts, then put away the foreign gods and the Ashtoreths from among you, and prepare your hearts for the Lord, and serve Him only; and He will deliver you from the hand of the Philistines.'" Take a closer look at what Samuel is telling them here because this has application for us as well. He laid out the path for restoration of their freedom and their peace. The first step: Return to the Lord. The obvious implication is that they had walked away from the Lord. The second step: Put away the idols. Apparently, they were clinging to the pagan gods of their neighbors instead of the Lord. The third step: Direct your hearts to the Lord. Be intentional about following the Lord. Then the fourth step: Serve the Lord only. He demands and deserves our exclusive worship. Samuel promised if they would do these four things, the Lord would deliver them.

For just a moment, think about what Samuel prescribed. Even though we may not refer to them as such, there are countless idols that people worship today. A host of addictions enslave multitudes.

Things that we put above God, and as a result, they control us. Perhaps there is something in your life that has you in bondage, keeping you from experiencing the fullness of God. Some challenge that is holding you back. These four steps work. Return to the Lord. Put away your idols. Whatever it is that you have put in the place of God, get rid of it. Direct your heart intentionally to the Lord and serve Him alone. There is no place for being double-minded. Either you are going to serve God or you are not.

Pay close attention to this next part in 1 Samuel 7:4–6: "So the children of Israel put away the Baals and the Ashtoreths, and served the LORD only. And Samuel said, 'Gather all Israel to Mizpah, and I will pray to the LORD for you.' So they gathered together at Mizpah, drew water, and poured it out before the LORD. And they fasted that day, and said there, 'We have sinned against the LORD.' And Samuel judged the children of Israel at Mizpah." The people responded to Samuel's altar call and he prayed for them.

However, just as they took this step of repentance in returning to the Lord, the predictable happened. The opposition showed up as we read in 1 Samuel 7:7–8: "Now when the Philistines heard that the children of Israel had gathered together at Mizpah, the lords of the Philistines went up against Israel. And when the children of Israel heard of it, they were afraid of the Philistines. So the children of Israel said to Samuel, 'Do not cease to cry out to the LORD our God for us, that He may save us from the hand of the Philistines.'" Frankly, this is often the case when we return to the Lord, leaving the forces of darkness behind that have enjoyed the influence over our lives. The fact is they do not want to let go. Consequently, when we begin that journey back to God, we often find it a struggle. We encounter opposition, which is designed to turn us again, away from God. Yet what we read here is encouraging. The people pressed into Samuel and pleaded, "Do not stop praying." That is what it takes.

As they prayed, the breakthrough came. Look at 1 Samuel 7:10–14:

> Now as Samuel was offering up the burnt offering, the Philistines drew near to battle against Israel. But the LORD thundered with a loud thunder upon the Philistines that day, and so confused them that they were overcome before Israel. And the men of Israel went out of Mizpah and pursued the Philistines, and drove them back as far as below Beth Car. Then Samuel took a stone and set it up between Mizpah and Shen, and called its name Ebenezer, saying, 'Thus far the LORD has helped us.' So the Philistines were subdued, and they did not come anymore into the territory of Israel. And the hand of the LORD was against the Philistines all the days of Samuel. Then the cities which the Philistines had taken from Israel were restored to Israel, from Ekron to Gath; and Israel recovered its territory from the hands of the Philistines. Also there was peace between Israel and the Amorites.

Repentance leads to restoration. What was restored to Israel? The Lord restored the land to them. The Lord also restored peace between Israel and the Amorites. When we are walking with God, even our enemies are at peace with us (Prov. 16:7).

Prayer

Father, thank You for Your Word. Lord, there is so much here that applies to us today. May the Holy Spirit continue to guide us, Lord, on this journey through Your Word that we will see and understand these principles, Lord, and that we will not find ourselves wanting to look to government to make up for our failure to obey You. Government can never do that. Of course, that is why we have such costly government and government that is such an overreach because we have refused to submit to You and to Your Word. We pray, Lord, as a nation, that You will bring us back to You and as individuals, that this nation might walk under Your blessing and under Your guidance. Again, we thank You, Lord, for Your Word, and we pray this in Jesus's name. Amen.

Questions for Reflection and Discussion

1. What test did the Philistines design to determine if the God of Israel was behind the plague that broke out among them (see 6:7–9)?

2. What did Samuel prescribe as the way of deliverance from the oppression of the Philistines (see 7:3)?

Notes on Today's Bible Reading

— Day 4 —

Today's Reading: 1 Samuel 8–10

Verse of the Day

> "But you have today rejected your God, who Himself saved you from all your adversities and your tribulations; and you have said to Him, 'No, set a king over us!'"
>
> *—1 Samuel 10:19*

Please read the entire Scripture selection in your own Bible and highlight or underline verses that stand out to you before you read the observations and engage the questions below.

Our study of 1 Samuel brings us to chapters 8–10 today. In these chapters, God gave the children of Israel what they thought they wanted: a king. Our key verse is 1 Samuel 10:19, "'But you have today rejected your God, who Himself saved you from all your adversities and your tribulations; and you have said to Him, "No, set a king over us!" Now therefore, present yourselves before the LORD by your tribes and by your clans.'"

For about 350 years, the twelve tribes of Israel were a loose confederation of tribes or states. They were a theocracy. Their relationship to God and their allegiance to His word was to be the glue that held them together. Yet as we see clearly in the book of Judges, they did not walk in the ways of God. Instead, every man did what was right in his own eyes. Consequently, God's hand of protection was removed and there was little unity to enable them to fend off their enemies. Indeed, they became vulnerable to attacks and adversaries. So, in these three chapters, we read of the transition from a theocracy to a monarchy as the people request and Samuel anoints Saul as Israel's first king. To be clear, a king could never relieve the people from their obligation to follow the law of the Lord. A king simply gave them a singular, visible leader designed to unify the twelve tribes into a single nation with the hopes that they might carry out God's instructions and keep His covenant.

Chapter 8 relates the people's request for a king. However, the chapter begins with the only reported blemish on Samuel's otherwise outstanding record of faithfulness. We read in 1 Samuel 8:1–3, "Now it came to pass when Samuel was old that he made his sons judges over Israel. The name of his firstborn was Joel, and the name of his second, Abijah; they were judges in Beersheba. But his sons did not walk in his ways; they turned aside after dishonest gain, took bribes, and perverted justice." It is important to point out a couple of truths here. First, our children have their own moral agency. In other words, they choose for themselves whether to obey or disobey and whom they will serve. However, second, parents in general and fathers in particular are accountable to teach their children to follow the Lord and walk in His ways.

Honestly, we anticipated that Samuel would have been overly sensitive to this responsibility of teaching his children to walk in the ways of God, given what he had witnessed with Eli and his two wayward sons. And perhaps he was sensitive and made the attempt. The record of Scripture does not give us a report other than to say that Samuel provided a godly example. If Samuel taught them to trust the Lord and walk in His ways as well as modeled that before them, the responsibility rests with his sons.

Unfortunately, some spiritual leaders become so focused on the church ministry or Christian organization that God has called them to that they neglect the first ministry to which God has called us, and that is to our families, to our wives and our children.

Believe me, I understand that no one is perfect. We all have our flaws. However, it goes back to being intentional and persistent, trying to do what God has called us to do with His help. Perhaps this was a blind spot in Samuel's life. We do not know. Again, we prefer to think Samuel was more in tune to this need because of the Eli experience. At the same time, this is a warning for all of us as fathers, as parents, that we need to be more intentional in teaching our children who the Lord is, what He has done for us, and what He requires from us.

Next consider 1 Samuel 8:4–6: "Then all the elders of Israel gathered together and came to Samuel at Ramah, and said to him, 'Look, you are old, and your sons do not walk in your ways. Now make us a king to judge us like all the nations.' But the thing displeased Samuel when they said, 'Give us a king to judge us.' So Samuel prayed to the LORD." Though he was irritated at their demand for a king, Samuel's response is a model for us. He took it to the Lord. Then the Lord answered in verses 7–8: "Heed the voice of the people in all that they say to you; for they have not rejected you, but they have rejected Me, that I should not reign over them. According to all the works which they have done since the day that I brought them up out of Egypt, even to this day—with which they have forsaken Me and served other gods—so they are doing to you also." God essentially said that this is their nature. This is who they are. This is what they do. Yet as with all things, God uses even our disobedience for His purposes.

Let us continue in 1 Samuel 8:9–11: "'Now therefore, heed their voice. However, you shall solemnly forewarn them, and show them the behavior of the king who will reign over them.' So Samuel told all the words of the LORD to the people who asked him for a king. And he said, 'This will be the behavior of the king who will reign over you: He will take your sons and appoint them for his own chariots and to be his horsemen, and some will run before his chariots.'" Samuel goes on to offer more of his warning about what will happen when they coronate a king to rule over them like the other nations (vv. 12–17). Bottom line: Having a king would cost them dearly, not only in terms of their finances but also in terms of their freedom.

In fact, the burden would be so heavy that they were going to cry out for relief as we read in verse 18: "'And you will cry out in that day because of your king whom you have chosen for yourselves, and the LORD will not hear you in that day.'" Do we see any application to political leaders in America? Absolutely. We must never put government in the place of God. The children of Israel were hoping for an easy way out because the consequences of disobeying God had led to their crisis situation where they were constantly being threatened by the enemies. They reasoned: "We will just get a king and we will be fine." But that is not the case. No form of government will work for a people who have rejected God as the ultimate Sovereign.

How did the children of Israel respond to God's warning though Samuel? We read in verses 19–20, "Nevertheless the people refused to obey the voice of Samuel; and they said, 'No, but we will have a king over us, that we also may be like all the nations, and that our king may judge us and go out before us and fight our battles.'" Again, they were not supposed to be like all the other nations. As a royal priesthood, a holy nation, we are not to be like everybody else. We are to be different from the world. That difference comes by obeying God and walking according to His word and His ways. Finally, in verses 21–22 we read, "And Samuel heard all the words of the people, and he repeated them in the hearing of the LORD. So the LORD said to Samuel, 'Heed their voice, and make them a king.' And Samuel said to the men of Israel, 'Every man go to his city.'"

Apparently, the people thought that the reason they were experiencing this political oppression, the reason they were being defeated by neighboring armies, the reason behind all their troubles was because of their form of government, the fact that they did not have a king. They failed to see that the problem was not the form of government. Whether a federation with judges, a monarchy with a king, or a republic with a president—or whatever form it might take—it is the character of the people, their obedience to and their dependence upon God, that determines their success more than anything else. It is a lesson for us.

In these next two chapters, God gave the Israelites what they were looking for in a king and what they would accept in a leader. The people got first pick, and they picked Saul. God got second pick, and he picked David. Unlike the people, God looked at the heart, the character of the person, but the people looked at the superficial qualities. That is why the Lord talked about Saul being taller, stronger, good looking, and more imposing among all the people because that is what the people were looking for in a king. They were looking for the superficial characteristics that they thought would bring success. By the way, that is generally how we pick our leaders today. Then we wonder why our nation is in trouble.

In chapter 9, we are introduced to the young man Saul, who was out looking for his father's donkeys. The story begins with a mundane family crisis, but it ends with Saul being anointed as Israel's first king. We begin in verses 1–3:

> There was a man of Benjamin whose name was Kish the son of Abiel, the son of Zeror, the son of Bechorath, the son of Aphiah, a Benjamite, a mighty man of power. And he had a choice and handsome son whose name was Saul. There was not a more handsome person than he among the children of Israel. From his shoulders upward he was taller than any of the people. Now the donkeys of Kish, Saul's father, were lost. And Kish said to his son Saul, "Please take one of the servants with you, and arise, go and look for the donkeys."

As we read further, we discover that Saul and the servants could not find the donkeys. From Saul's perspective, this must have seemed like a failed mission. From God's perspective, it was His divine providence working to bring Saul to exactly the right city at exactly the right time to meet the prophet Samuel. Have you ever felt like you are in the middle of a "donkey hunt"? Pursuing a task that seems trivial, frustrating, or even pointless? God often uses such searches to relocate us to where He wants us to be. Your current frustration may actually be a divine appointment in disguise.

Indeed, just when Saul was about to give up and head back home, the story turns when his servant essentially suggests in verse 6, "Hey, we are close to the city where there is a man of God. Let us go and enlist his help." We read the account of the God-arranged meeting in 1 Samuel 9:14–21:

> So they went up to the city. As they were coming into the city, there was Samuel, coming out toward them on his way up to the high place. Now the Lord had told Samuel in his ear the day before Saul came, saying, "Tomorrow about this time I will send you a man from the land of Benjamin, and you shall anoint him commander over My people Israel, that he may save My people from the hand of the Philistines; for I have looked upon My people, because their cry has come to Me." So when Samuel saw Saul, the Lord said to him, "There he is, the man of whom I spoke to you. This one shall reign over My people." Then Saul drew near to Samuel in the gate, and said, "Please tell me, where is the seer's house?" Samuel answered Saul and said, "I am the seer. Go up before me to the high place, for you shall eat with me today; and tomorrow I will let you go and will tell you all that is in your heart. But as for your donkeys that were lost three days ago, do not be anxious about them, for they have been found. And on whom is all the desire of Israel? Is it not on you and on all your father's house?" And Saul answered and said, "Am I not a Benjamite, of the smallest of the tribes of Israel, and my family the least

> of all the families of the tribe of Benjamin? Why then do you speak like this to me?"

God had divinely engineered this entire encounter. Years before this episode, the tribe of Benjamin had almost been exterminated because of the wickedness that occurred in Gibeah (see Judges 20). This too may have been a factor in the selection of Saul. Tribes that were often suspicious and jealous of one another would not have been overly concerned about this tiny tribe of Benjamin amassing too much power. Again, God was selecting the leader that the people wanted. Consequently, that was the reason Saul was put forward.

In chapter 10, Samuel gave Saul the word of the Lord, anointed him, and gave him three signs that confirmed the word of the Lord. These three signs were fulfilled in this chapter. Look at 1 Samuel 10:1–5:

> Then Samuel took a flask of oil and poured it on his head, and kissed him and said: "Is it not because the LORD has anointed you commander over His inheritance? When you have departed from me today, you will find two men by Rachel's tomb in the territory of Benjamin at Zelzah; and they will say to you, 'The donkeys which you went to look for have been found. And now your father has ceased caring about the donkeys and is worrying about you, saying, "What shall I do about my son?"' Then you shall go on forward from there and come to the terebinth tree of Tabor. There three men going up to God at Bethel will meet you, one carrying three young goats, another carrying three loaves of bread, and another carrying a skin of wine. And they will greet you and give you two loaves of bread, which you shall receive from their hands. After that you shall come to the hill of God where the Philistine garrison is. And it will happen, when you have come there to the city,

> that you will meet a group of prophets coming down from the high place with a stringed instrument, a tambourine, a flute, and a harp before them; and they will be prophesying."

Samuel was extremely specific in his prophetic description of what was about to happen, so there would be no room for misinterpreting it.

Let us continue in 1 Samuel 10:6–7: "'Then the Spirit of the LORD will come upon you, and you will prophesy with them and be turned into another man. And let it be, when these signs come to you, that you do as the occasion demands; for God is with you.'" The spirit of the Lord would come upon Saul, and he would be turned into another man. This is the power of the Holy Spirit. Now in the Old Testament, the anointing of the Holy Spirit was generally for a specific task or office. But as believers, as followers of Jesus Christ, we receive the Holy Spirit when we believe and confess faith in Jesus Christ, which provides us with the power to be witnesses for Christ, bringing glory to the Father, which is our task now. The Holy Spirit in the Old Testament provides what is needed based upon what the occasion demands, as we read here for Saul. Now remember Jesus told His disciples, and us by extension, not to worry about what to say when we are hauled before hostile powers because it will be given to us in that hour, and we will know what to say. The Holy Spirit will provide what the occasion demands (see Matt. 10:19–20).

Continue to 1 Samuel 10:9: "So it was, when he had turned his back to go from Samuel, that God gave him another heart; and all those signs came to pass that day." God confirmed all that Samuel had told Saul, and we read that God gave Saul another heart. So does that mean Saul was saved? Was he redeemed by faith in God like Abraham? I have to say, I do not know. If we simply look at the fruit, we will soon see that Saul did not operate in faith and obedience. In fact, it was just the opposite. There are several figures in the Old Testament that are truly difficult to figure out, and Saul is certainly one of those.

Next we read in 1 Samuel 10:17–19: "Then Samuel called the people together to the Lord at Mizpah, and said to the children of Israel, 'Thus says the Lord God of Israel: "I brought up Israel out of Egypt, and delivered you from the hand of the Egyptians and from the hand of all kingdoms and from those who oppressed you." But you have today rejected your God, who Himself saved you from all your adversities and your tribulations; and you have said to Him, "No, set a king over us!" Now therefore, present yourselves before the Lord by your tribes and by your clans.'"

They had a theocracy. God was at the head of the nation. They were to walk in His ways. Yet they rejected God as their King. In their rebellion, they wanted a human king instead, like the nations around them, thinking that would solve all their problems. Well, as we will soon discover, it did not work.

Then in verses 20–21, we read of the formal selection process, which was by lot. Yet when Saul was chosen, he was actually hiding in the equipment—or as the old King James put it, the baggage. However, God calls Saul out, and he is then presented to the people in verse 24: "And Samuel said to all the people, 'Do you see him whom the Lord has chosen, that there is no one like him among all the people?' So all the people shouted and said, 'Long live the king!'" They had the candidate that met their criteria, and Samuel again tells them the cost of their choice. We read in verses 25–27, "Then Samuel explained to the people the behavior of royalty, and wrote it in a book"—Right? He wrote it down so they couldn't deny that he had warned them—"and laid it up before the Lord. And Samuel sent all the people away, every man to his house. And Saul also went to Gibeah; and valiant men went with him, whose hearts God had touched. But some rebels said, 'How can this man save us?' So they despised him, and brought him no presents. But he held his peace."

This final verse is instructive. In every age, there are rebels. Every leader will have their detractors. Yet ultimately, it is the rejection of God. Not only are they rejecting the leader, but ultimately, they are rebelling against God, who delegates authority. There are exceptions to be sure. During the American Revolution, the motto "Rebellion to Tyrants is Obedience to God" was part of a design considered for our national seal by no less than Ben Franklin and Thomas Jefferson. We all understand what Peter meant when he declared, "We ought to obey God rather than men" (Acts 5:29). Yet for some, rebellion has nothing to do with obedience to God. It is rebellion for rebellion's sake. What Saul did here in the initial stage of his kingship, his monarchy, was actually a display of wisdom. He lets God deal with them. Honestly, that is the best thing to do with our detractors. When God positions you in a place of leadership, you are going to have detractors. It is simply ingrained into the nature of fallen man. Take counsel from this passage. Let God deal with them.

Prayer

Father, thank You for Your Word. And Lord, as we continue on this journey, may the Holy Spirit open our eyes, our understanding, and our hearts to receive Your truth. That we will go beyond just looking at this as a historical account of what happened to the children of Israel and instead that we will glean from this the principles that apply to our lives each and every day. Give us wisdom, Lord. Give us knowledge and understanding, which comes from Your Word. We pray and ask this in Jesus's name. Amen.

Questions for Reflection and Discussion

1. What did Samuel tell Saul would happen, and what did happen that prepared Saul to become the leader of Israel (see 10:2–13)?

2. What caused the valiant men to follow Saul (see 10:26)?

Notes on Today's Bible Reading

— Day 5 —

Today's Reading: 1 Samuel 11–13

Verse of the Day

> "If you fear the Lord and serve Him and obey His voice, and do not rebel against the commandment of the Lord, then both you and the king who reigns over you will continue following the Lord your God."
>
> —*1 Samuel 12:14*

Please read the entire Scripture selection in your own Bible and highlight or underline verses that stand out to you before you read the observations and engage the questions below.

Today we consider 1 Samuel 11–13. Our key verse is 1 Samuel 12:14, which says, "'If you fear the Lord and serve Him and obey His voice, and do not rebel against the commandment of the Lord, then both you and the king who reigns over you will continue following the Lord your God.'" These chapters detail the establishment of Saul's monarchy, moving from his successful military debut to his first major failure. In chapter 11, Saul unites Israel to defeat the Ammonites, leading to his official coronation. In chapter 12, Samuel delivers his "Farewell Address," in which he defends his integrity, warns against disobedience, and reaffirms the covenant. In chapter 13, Saul disobeys God by offering sacrifices himself, instead of waiting for Samuel, and in the end loses his dynasty.

In chapter 11, we see Saul in his first military action as the Ammonites make a move on Jabesh Gilead, which was the area of the half tribe of Manasseh on the east side of the Jordan River. The tribes had not yet unified. Saul was kind of a king-in-name-only, a king in waiting. The Ammonites thought Jabesh Gilead would be easy pickings because they were separated from the rest of the tribes by the Jordan River. Plus, the tribes west of the river had their own issues with the Philistines. However, Nahash, the Ammonite leader, miscalculated.

Begin in 1 Samuel 11:1: "Then Nahash the Ammonite came up and encamped against Jabesh Gilead; and all the men of Jabesh said to Nahash, 'Make a covenant with us, and we will serve you.'" The Israelites were ready to wave a white flag of surrender, at least the half tribe of Manasseh, until they heard the terms. Look at verse 2: "And Nahash the Ammonite answered them, 'On this condition I will make a covenant with you, that I may put out all your right eyes, and bring reproach on all Israel.'" Obviously, that would be humiliating. Remember, Samson? They plucked out his eyes. It would also have the practical effect of rendering the men useless as warriors because they actually carried their shield with their left hand and looked around it with their right eye. Consequently, the elders of the city made a request of the Ammonite leader in verse 3: "'Hold off for seven days, that we may send messengers to all the territory of Israel. And then, if there is no one to save us, we will come out to you.'" Now, I assume that they thought appealing to the other tribes was worth a try. If nothing else, it would buy them some time.

Word reaches the new king, as we read in 1 Samuel 11:4–6: "So the messengers came to Gibeah of Saul and told the news in the hearing of the people. And all the people lifted up their voices and wept. Now there was Saul, coming behind the herd from the field; and Saul said, 'What troubles the people, that they weep?' And they told him the words of the men of Jabesh. Then the Spirit of God came upon Saul when he heard this news, and his anger was greatly aroused." What Saul demonstrated here is what we call righteous indignation. This anger was not sparked by some personal slight. This was about God and His people. It was the same thing that happened when Jesus turned over the tables in the temple. It wasn't about Him; it was about God's house. It was about the reputation of the Father. Saul's next move was quite dramatic in verse 7: "So he took a yoke of oxen and cut them in pieces, and sent them throughout all the territory of Israel by the hands of messengers, saying, 'Whoever does not go out with Saul and Samuel to battle, so it shall be done to his oxen.' And the fear of the Lord fell on the people, and they came out with one consent." This sounds familiar, does it not? Bold action prompts more action. We see this repeatedly in Scripture.

Drop down to verses 11–13: "So it was, on the next day, that Saul put the people in three companies; and they came into the midst of the camp in the morning watch, and killed Ammonites until the heat of the day. And it happened that those who survived were scattered, so that no two of them were left together. Then the people said to Samuel, 'Who is he who said, "Shall Saul reign over us?" Bring the men, that we may put them to death.' But Saul said, 'Not a man shall be put to death this day, for today the Lord has accomplished salvation in Israel.'" At the height of his first triumph, Saul resisted the urge to settle old scores. He declared, "[T]oday the Lord has accomplished salvation in Israel," declining any glory for himself and shifting it all toward God. If only Saul had remained that type of king and not the petty one he will become as we will read about shortly.

In chapter 12, Samuel's time as judge of Israel was coming to a close. Like every good leader that came before him, Samuel gives a history lesson, a refresher course on who God is, what God had done for them, and what God expected from them. Look at 1 Samuel 12:1–2: "Now Samuel said to all Israel: 'Indeed I have heeded your voice in all that you said to me, and have made a king over you. And now here is the king, walking before you; and I am old and grayheaded, and look, my sons are with you. I have walked before you from my childhood to this day.'" Samuel went on to talk about how he had served them selflessly, vindicating his own integrity and challenging anyone to find an instance where he cheated or oppressed them. His leadership wasn't based on a title but on a lifetime of "clean hands." He could face the people boldly because he had never used his position for personal gain. The people agreed with his assessment.

Continue with 1 Samuel 12:6–7: "Then Samuel said to the people, 'It is the LORD who raised up Moses and Aaron, and who brought your fathers up from the land of Egypt. Now therefore, stand still, that I may reason with you before the LORD concerning all the righteous acts of the LORD which He did to you and your fathers.'" So he begins this history lesson.

Look at 1 Samuel 12:12–14: "'And when you saw that Nahash king of the Ammonites came against you, you said to me, "No, but a king shall reign over us," when the LORD your God was your king. Now therefore, here is the king whom you have chosen and whom you have desired. And take note, the LORD has set a king over you. If you fear the LORD and serve Him and obey His voice, and do not rebel against the commandment of the LORD, then both you and the king who reigns over you will continue following the LORD your God.'" So again, a king does not exempt the people from obeying God and walking in the ways of God. I mean, here's an uncomfortable truth: Our leaders reflect who we are collectively. This requires both the leaders and the people to walk with the Lord. If the people are godly, the nation will have godly leadership. I know we get really frustrated, irate, and even angry over the corrupt, immoral leadership that we have in our nation, but it is a reflection of who we have become as a people. And so, we have to do our part. And you might say, "Well, I cannot control what is happening." You do not have to control what you cannot control. God is number one. Your responsibility is your family and those you influence. And we are called to be salt, called to be light. We are called to be influences right where God has placed us. So, we take our responsibility seriously and collectively, as we do that, we can change the country.

Look at 1 Samuel 12:15: "'However, if you do not obey the voice of the LORD, but rebel against the commandment of the LORD, then the hand of the LORD will be against you, as it was against your fathers.'" So he's saying, "Do not think just because you have a king, you have got an excuse to do what you want and blame it on the king, and vice versa." Let us continue in 1 Samuel 12:16–18: "'Now therefore, stand and see this great thing which the LORD will do before your eyes: Is today not the wheat harvest? I will call to the LORD, and He will send thunder and rain, that you may perceive and see that your wickedness is great, which you have done in the sight of the LORD, in asking a king for yourselves.' So Samuel called to the LORD, and the LORD sent thunder and rain that day; and all the people greatly feared the LORD and Samuel." Remember, the king was not God's plan. It was not God's plan for them because, again, they just did not want to follow God's rules. And they thought, *Well, you know, all of these bad things that are happening to us because we are not obeying God, if we just had a king that could lead us, we could offset that.* That is one of the reasons we have nearly $34 trillion in debt as a nation; we feel like we can just give government more responsibility and we can do what we want. Government can never mitigate the consequences of sin.

Let us continue in 1 Samuel 12:19–21: "And all the people said to Samuel, 'Pray for your servants to the LORD your God, that we may not die; for we have added to all our sins the evil of asking a king for ourselves.' Then Samuel said to the people, 'Do not fear. You have done all this wickedness; yet do not turn aside from following the LORD, but serve the LORD with all your heart. And do not turn aside; for then you would go after empty things which cannot profit or deliver, for they are nothing.'" Yet again, Samuel calls them out for idol worship and the wickedness associated with it. Why did they worship idols? Because they thought they could mold them into something that affirmed what they wanted, so that worship sanctioned sin. That is what idols do. Specifically, the sexual immorality associated with the worship of idols allowed them to participate in it and call it worship.

However, Samuel not only had a hard word; he also had a gracious word in 1 Samuel 12:22: "'For the LORD will not forsake His people, for His great name's sake, because it has pleased the LORD to make you His people.'" How refreshing to know that despite our sin, God is willing to forgive and restore. He will not forsake His people. Samuel adds in verse 23, "'Moreover, as for me, far be it from me that I should sin against the LORD in ceasing to pray for you; but I will teach you the good and the right way.'" Now here is an admirable character trait of a godly leader, who had been pushed away by the people as they sought their king. Despite their rejection, Samuel made a commitment: "I will continue to pray for you and teach you the right way." When our children rebel and seem to reject our spiritual leadership, follow Samuel's example. Keep praying for them. Keep teaching them the right way. He concludes with a summary in verses 24–25: "'Only fear the LORD, and serve Him in truth with all your heart; for consider what great things He has done for you. But if you still do wickedly, you shall be swept away, both you and your king.'" He's teaching them how to maintain a right relationship with the Lord, which is the pathway to blessing. However, he also teaches them about the peril of rebellion and wickedness.

In chapter 13, we find Israel in a desperate state. The Philistines had gathered a massive army, prompting the Israelites to hide out of terror. Saul gathered his army at Gilgal, waiting for the prophet Samuel to arrive and offer a sacrifice before battle. However, Samuel had instructed Saul to wait seven days. As the deadline passed and his troops began to desert him in fear, Saul took matters into his own hands. He offered the burnt offering himself, which is the role and responsibility strictly reserved for the priests. Perhaps his early success had gone to his head, and his humility had turned to pride. Or perhaps he simply panicked. Regardless, this moment marked the beginning of the end for Saul. When Samuel finally arrived, he was filled with righteous indignation, as we read in 1 Samuel 13:11–14:

> And Samuel said, "What have you done?" Saul said, "When I saw that the people were scattered from me, and that you did not come within the days appointed, and that the Philistines gathered together at Michmash, then I said, 'The Philistines will now come down on me at Gilgal, and I have not made supplication to the LORD.' Therefore I felt compelled, and offered a burnt offering." And Samuel said to Saul, "You have done foolishly. You have not kept the commandment of the LORD your God, which He commanded you. For now the LORD would have established your kingdom over Israel forever. But now your kingdom shall not continue. The LORD has sought for Himself a man after His own heart, and the LORD has commanded him to be commander over His people, because you have not kept what the LORD commanded you."

Here we witness a defining moment in King Saul's reign where his internal character was tested by an external crisis. Having to wait is often a test of our faith and our obedience. Unfortunately, Saul failed. He failed to wait on the Lord and follow specific instructions regarding sacrifices. Instead, Saul chose expedience over obedience. It is a reminder to treat God's Word with weight and not just assume that a good intention or a pressing situation justifies a direct violation of His commands. Yet hope was on the horizon. The Lord had a worthy successor, a "man after His own heart."

The rest of the chapter speaks to another topic, what I call the purpose of disarming a population. The Philistines had taken away all the weapons and even the means to manufacture them. Look at 1 Samuel 13:19–22:

> Now there was no blacksmith to be found throughout all the land of Israel, for the Philistines said, "Lest the Hebrews make swords or spears." But all the Israelites would go down to the Philistines to sharpen each man's plowshare, his mattock, his ax, and his sickle; and the charge for a sharpening was a pim for the plowshares, the mattocks, the forks, and the axes, and to set the points of the goads. So it came about, on the day of battle, that there was neither sword nor spear found in the hand of any of the people who were with Saul and Jonathan. But they were found with Saul and Jonathan his son.

How discouraging are these concluding verses? The Israelites even had to take their farming tools to the Philistines for sharpening. No one had weapons except the king and his son. Such was the desperate military state of Israel following Saul's disobedience.

Prayer

Father, thank You for Your Word. We thank You for the truths that are in it, both the encouragement and the warnings. We thank You for the example of Samuel, his integrity and his commitment to prayer. May we take warning from the example of Saul, who chose expedience over obedience. Once again, we ask the Holy Spirit to lead us in our understanding of Your Word and how we are to apply it to our lives. Lord, may we walk in obedience to You. We pray in Jesus's name. Amen.

Questions for Reflection and Discussion

1. What stirred up the anger of Saul over the threat to the people of Jabesh Gilead (see 11:1–6)?

2. What did Samuel tell the people to do if they did not want to be swept away by God for doing wickedness (see 12:24–25)?

Notes on Today's Bible Reading

— Day 6 —

Today's Reading: 1 Samuel 14

Verse of the Day

> Then Jonathan said to the young man who bore his armor, "Come, let us go over to the garrison of these uncircumcised; it may be that the LORD will work for us. For nothing restrains the LORD from saving by many or by few."
>
> *—1 Samuel 14:6*

Please read the entire Scripture selection in your own Bible and highlight or underline verses that stand out to you before you read the observations and engage the questions below.

Today we study 1 Samuel 14, and we begin with a question: What is the difference between having faith in God and being spiritual? That is one of several things we find in 1 Samuel 14. After reading about Saul's reign to this point, it is fair to conclude that little had changed for the Israelites. They remained under the oppression of the Philistines. In fact, it was even worse than before they had a king because they had no weapons with which to fight. The chapter opens with Saul sitting under a pomegranate tree with his dwindling, weaponless army while his son Jonathan is on the move. Jonathan decides that God doesn't need an army to win a battle with the enemy and takes action. Saul and Jonathan present a stark contrast between the paralysis of fear on one hand and the initiative of faith on the other.

You have to admire the courage of Jonathan in 1 Samuel 14:1: "Now it happened one day that Jonathan the son of Saul said to the young man who bore his armor, 'Come, let us go over to the Philistines' garrison that is on the other side.' But he did not tell his father." How bold for two men to approach the enemy camp! Jonathan took this initiative based on his faith in the Lord as we read in verse 6: "Then Jonathan said to the young man who bore his armor, 'Come, let us go over to the garrison of these uncircumcised; it may be that the LORD will work for us. For nothing restrains the LORD from saving by many or by few.'" Please do not miss this. Faith is on the move. Consider Jonathan's insightful and, arguably, logical understanding of God's power—if it is the power of God that delivers. Whether it is by the hand of many or a few, God will bring about the victory. That is something we need to remember. If we are really trusting in God, then quite frankly, the circumstances do not matter. It is our obedience and our trust in Him that makes the difference.

Look at 1 Samuel 14:11–12: "So both of them showed themselves to the garrison of the Philistines. And the Philistines said, 'Look, the Hebrews are coming out of the holes where they have hidden.' Then the men of the garrison called to Jonathan and his armorbearer, and said, 'Come up to us, and we will show you something.' Jonathan said to his armorbearer, 'Come up after me, for the LORD has delivered them into the hand of Israel.'" What the Philistines were basically saying, "Come up, we will teach you a thing or two." Yet when we are on the side of the Lord, the intimidating words of the opposition are meaningless. Jonathan actually saw that because he had laid out a fleece before the LORD. He said, "If they say come up, then that means the LORD wants us to come up." So, the words of intimidation that the enemy put forth were actually the invitation of God to move out in faith.

Look at 1 Samuel 14:13–15: "And Jonathan climbed up on his hands and knees with his armorbearer after him; and they fell before Jonathan. And as he came after him, his armorbearer killed them.

That first slaughter which Jonathan and his armorbearer made was about twenty men within about half an acre of land. And there was trembling in the camp, in the field, and among all the people. The garrison and the raiders also trembled; and the earth quaked, so that it was a very great trembling." This is another example of God using the forces of creation, which He controls for His purposes based upon the faith of a man. Now, this sounds like Jesus over in Matthew 21:21: "So Jesus answered and said to them, 'Assuredly, I say to you, if you have faith and do not doubt, you will not only do what was done to the fig tree, but also if you say to this mountain, "Be removed and be cast into the sea," it will be done.'" Our faith cannot only move mountains, but it can shake them as well.

Now juxtapose the faith of Jonathan to the spirituality of Saul. Look at 1 Samuel 14:18: "And Saul said to Ahijah, 'Bring the ark of God here' (for at that time the ark of God was with the children of Israel)." Now there is debate about this move by Saul. Some see it as a genuine attempt to inquire of the Lord. Others see it as the same superstitious attitude the Israelites had about the ark when they faced off with the Philistines back in chapter 4. Remember, when Eli was the priest and it was captured by the Philistines, they had treated the ark not as the place of God's holy presence but basically as a good-luck charm. Saul's motives are unclear at this point, but his request begs the question.

Perhaps his next move will help us toward a conclusion. In 1 Samuel 14:24 we read, "And the men of Israel were distressed that day, for Saul had placed the people under oath, saying, 'Cursed is the man who eats any food until evening, before I have taken vengeance on my enemies.' So none of the people tasted food." Now, that was a reckless use of spiritual things to either gain the favor of God or look spiritual in the eyes of others. Fasting is an expression of our dependence upon God; it is not intended to gratify the ambitions of a king. Yes, there is a time to fast, but it is not in the midst of a battle when strength is needed.

Jonathan understood this. In fact, we read in 1 Samuel 14:27–32,

> But Jonathan had not heard his father charge the people with the oath; therefore he stretched out the end of the rod that was in his hand and dipped it in a honeycomb, and put his hand to his mouth; and his countenance brightened. Then one of the people said, "Your father strictly charged the people with an oath, saying, 'Cursed is the man who eats food this day.'" And the people were faint. But Jonathan said, "My father has troubled the land. Look now, how my countenance has brightened because I tasted a little of this honey. How much better if the people had eaten freely today of the spoil of their enemies which they found! For now would there not have been a much greater slaughter among the Philistines?" Now they had driven back the Philistines that day from Michmash to Aijalon. So the people were very faint. And the people rushed on the spoil, and took sheep, oxen, and calves, and slaughtered them on the ground; and the people ate them with the blood.

Now the rash vow of Saul led to starving men, violating a prohibition in God's law against consuming raw meat with the blood. As we read on, we find yet another rash vow of Saul, which again appeared to be an effort to look spiritual as opposed to acting with faith, as Jonathan had done. He had put them into a posture of having to obey an order of a man and violate the law of God, the clear direction of God. We see here again the faith of Jonathan juxtaposed to the spirituality of Saul. God doesn't want us to be spiritual. God wants us to operate in faith.

Prayer

Father, we thank You for Your Word. Thank You, Lord, for Your blessings. We pray, Father God, for Your direction upon our lives. May we learn from Scripture. May we learn from Your Word how to operate in faith, not being spiritual in the eyes of others, but Lord, having faith in Your presence. We pray in Jesus's name. Amen.

Questions for Reflection and Discussion

1. Jonathan's confidence that he and his armorbearer could successfully take on a more significant number of Philistines was based upon (see 14:6):
   a. His and his armorbearer's ability
   b. A dream that he had
   c. The power of God
   d. All the above

2. What does this passage teach us about making vows or oaths (see 14:24–28)?

Notes on Today's Bible Reading

— Day 7 —

Today's Reading: 1 Samuel 15–16

Verse of the Day

> But the LORD said to Samuel, "Do not look at his appearance or at his physical stature, because I have refused him. For the LORD does not see as man sees; for man looks at the outward appearance, but the LORD looks at the heart."
>
> *—1 Samuel 16:7*

Please read the entire Scripture selection in your own Bible and highlight or underline verses that stand out to you before you read the observations and engage the questions below.

Today our study brings us to 1 Samuel 15–16. These two chapters are rich with relevant principles for our lives. Our key verse is 1 Samuel 16:7: "But the LORD said to Samuel, 'Do not look at his appearance or at his physical stature, because I have refused him. For the LORD does not see as man sees; for man looks at the outward appearance, but the LORD looks at the heart.'" In chapter 15, Saul finally crosses the line, and God tells him, "You are done." Then in chapter 16, we have Samuel's one-man search team, and it is being directed by the Lord to look at an unlikely candidate, a young man named David.

We begin in 1 Samuel 15:1: "Samuel also said to Saul, 'The LORD sent me to anoint you king over His people, over Israel. Now therefore, heed the voice of the words of the LORD.'" Please do not miss the obvious application. It is not enough to hear the word of the Lord. You have to act upon it. You have to obey it. James famously put it this way: "But be doers of the word, and not hearers only, deceiving yourselves" (Jas. 1:22). That is what it means to "heed the voice of the words of the LORD."

Continue in 1 Samuel 15:2–3: "'Thus says the LORD of hosts: "I will punish Amalek for what he did to Israel, how he ambushed him on the way when he came up from Egypt. Now go and attack Amalek, and utterly destroy all that they have, and do not spare them. But kill both man and woman, infant and nursing child, ox and sheep, camel and donkey."'" How well did Saul "heed the voice of the words of the LORD"? We find out in 1 Samuel 15:8–9: "He also took Agag king of the Amalekites alive, and utterly destroyed all the people with the edge of the sword. But Saul and the people spared Agag and the best of the sheep, the oxen, the fatlings, the lambs, and all that was good, and were unwilling to utterly destroy them. But everything despised and worthless, that they utterly destroyed." Here is the takeaway: Partial obedience is not obedience. In fact, it is merely disobedience.

Continue in 1 Samuel 15:10–11: "Now the word of the LORD came to Samuel, saying, 'I greatly regret that I have set up Saul as king, for he has turned back from following Me, and has not performed My commandments.' And it grieved Samuel, and he cried out to the LORD all night." The Lord admits that He regretted making Saul the king, and this raises an interesting question. Can men who go bad cause God to alter His course? We know that God's purposes will be accomplished. Nothing will frustrate the plans of God. Yet does the free will of man influence God's plans? We will leave it there for meditation. What we can comprehend is Samuel's response: He laments. He weeps. He prays. He cried out to the Lord all night long. Even though Samuel was not in favor of coronating a king and establishing the monarchy, he was grieved by

God's announcement and interceded throughout the night. This is a powerful example for us as servants of God. Samuel was grieved by God's announcement that he was rejecting Saul, and so he interceded throughout the night. This is an example of being empty of self in yielding to God and His purposes. I truly admire Samuel and his selfless, God-centered heart. Frankly, I have been challenged to seek the Lord to become this kind of leader. I pray it will challenge you as well.

Continue in 1 Samuel 15:12: "So when Samuel rose early in the morning to meet Saul, it was told Samuel, saying, 'Saul went to Carmel, and indeed, he set up a monument for himself; and he has gone on around, passed by, and gone down to Gilgal.'" This is a sure sign of a pending fall. Building monuments for yourself is not a good thing. Look at 1 Samuel 15:13–15: "Then Samuel went to Saul, and Saul said to him, 'Blessed are you of the LORD! I have performed the commandment of the LORD.' But Samuel said, 'What then is this bleating of the sheep in my ears, and the lowing of the oxen which I hear?' And Saul said, 'They have brought them from the Amalekites; for the people spared the best of the sheep and the oxen, to sacrifice to the LORD your God; and the rest we have utterly destroyed.'" This was more rationalizing and attempts to justify disobedience. They said, "I know what you told us God said, but we figured he would appreciate a few nice sheep."

Not surprisingly, Samuel was not convinced as we read in 1 Samuel 15:18–21:

> "Now the LORD sent you on a mission, and said, 'Go, and utterly destroy the sinners, the Amalekites, and fight against them until they are consumed.' Why then did you not obey the voice of the LORD? Why did you swoop down on the spoil, and do evil in the sight of the LORD?" And Saul said to Samuel, "But I have obeyed the voice of the LORD, and gone on the mission on which the LORD sent me, and brought back

> Agag king of Amalek; I have utterly destroyed the Amalekites. But the people took of the plunder, sheep and oxen, the best of the things which should have been utterly destroyed, to sacrifice to the LORD your God in Gilgal."

This was a clear sign that Saul was not a God-oriented leader. Look how quickly he pushed the blame onto the people he was supposed to be leading. Real leaders take responsibility.

Next, we read a familiar and important Scripture:

> So Samuel said:
> "Has the LORD as great delight in burnt offerings
> and sacrifices,
> As in obeying the voice of the LORD?
> Behold, to obey is better than sacrifice,
> And to heed than the fat of rams.
> For rebellion is as the sin of witchcraft,
> And stubbornness is as iniquity and idolatry.
> Because you have rejected the word of the LORD,
> He also has rejected you from being king." (vv. 22–23)

What does God value most? Here it is in this text: obedience. It is not what you do for Him, not what you offer Him, but rather your obedience to Him. But do not miss this last part. Saul rejected the word of God, and as a result, God rejected him.

Next note Saul's response in 1 Samuel 15:24: "Then Saul said to Samuel, 'I have sinned, for I have transgressed the commandment of the LORD and your words, because I feared the people and obeyed their voice.'" After having this sentence passed on him, Saul shows remorse. Samuel's pronouncement of judgment got his attention. What Saul said next is revealing; do not miss this. He claimed, "I did it because I feared the people." Disobedience to God or failure to fully obey is often rooted in the fear of man, which never has a good outcome. This is why God called Joshua to lead. He gave him the instructions to be strong and courageous. Joshua 1:7 says, "Only be strong and very courageous, that you may observe to do according to all the law which Moses My servant commanded you; do not turn from it to the right hand or to the left, that you may prosper wherever you go." You see, courage is needed to obey the voice of God in the sight of man. Today that is especially true. We need to be praying for courage to live out the truth of God's Word in a culture that is increasingly rejecting the truth of God.

In chapter 16, the narrative shifts from the failing reign of Saul to the secret anointing of a shepherd boy. The Lord sends Samuel to Bethlehem, to the house of Jesse. When Samuel arrives, he sees Eliab, the eldest son, who is tall and handsome, exactly what a king should look like. Samuel thinks in verse 6, "'Surely the Lord's anointed is before Him!'" But God corrects him with one of the most famous lines in Scripture: "But the Lord said to Samuel, 'Do not look at his appearance or at his physical stature, because I have refused him. For the Lord does not see as man sees; for man looks at the outward appearance, but the Lord looks at the heart'" (v. 7). He goes through all the sons of Jesse who are present. Seven brothers pass by, and seven times God says no. You can almost read the puzzlement in Samuel's voice when he asks in verse 11, "'Are all the young men here?'" Jesse replied, "'There remains yet the youngest, and there he is, keeping the sheep.'" Samuel then directed Jesse to call his youngest, and we read in verse 12, "So he sent and brought him in. Now he was ruddy, with bright eyes, and good-looking. And the Lord said, 'Arise, anoint him; for this is the one!'"

There are three truths to consider by way of takeaway from this episode. First, the heart is what qualifies a leader. While the world hires based on résumés and follows based on charisma, God calls based on the condition of the heart. David was a man after God's own heart. Second, private faithfulness precedes public calling. God shaped and molded David away from the public eye while he tended sheep, fighting off predators, providing water and pasture, keeping his charge. He was faithful over a little; God was about to make him ruler over much. Third, God's presence is the evidence of His calling. We see this down in 1 Samuel 16:13–14: "Then Samuel took the horn of oil and anointed him in the midst of his brothers; and the Spirit of the LORD came upon David from that day forward. So Samuel arose and went to Ramah. But the Spirit of the LORD departed from Saul, and a distressing spirit from the LORD troubled him."

Note the contrast there. A distressing spirit came upon Saul, but the Spirit of the Lord came upon David. Interestingly, this development in Saul's life was part of God's providential plan to have David introduced to the royal court, as we see in 1 Samuel 16:14–23. Saul's anguish prompted him to ask his servants to bring in a musician. A servant put forward David: "'Look, I have seen a son of Jesse the Bethlehemite, who is skillful in playing, a mighty man of valor, a man of war, prudent in speech, and a handsome person; and the LORD is with him'" (v. 18). When David came, Saul took an immediate liking to David and made him his armorbearer. Whenever the distressing spirit afflicted Saul, David played the lyre, providing temporary relief and causing the spirit to depart. We will see more of the internal battle within Saul as we read further.

Back when Samuel anointed David, the Holy Spirit came upon him from that point forward. Honestly, we have neglected the understanding of the power of the Holy Spirit, maybe out of fear of those who associate the Holy Spirit with certain spiritual experiences. In the Old Testament, the Holy Spirit was more associated with a position or with an assignment. It was selective and it was temporary. Under the new covenant, we receive the Holy Spirit when we accept Jesus Christ as our Lord and Savior. However, we choose whether we will be filled with the Holy Spirit or not, meaning whether we will be controlled by the Holy Spirit and whether He will govern our lives. Paul says in Ephesians 5:18, "And do not be drunk with wine, in which is dissipation; but be filled with the Spirit." The question is, Will it be the influence of the world or the influence of the Holy Spirit that directs our steps? The power of the Holy Spirit has not diminished since the Old Testament. We, as believers, have access to the same power that God anointed His servants with in the Old Testament. It is universal to us as we accept Jesus Christ as our Savior because we are His anointed servants. We are here to do His work, His mission. We need to walk in that power and pursue His mission and purpose that He has given us.

Prayer

Father, thank You for Your Word, and Lord, may we heed it. May we not just listen and then do what we want to do. But Lord, may we listen, may we heed, may we obey Your Word. And may the power of the Holy Spirit be upon our lives—guiding us, directing us, changing us, transforming us, using us for the mission to which You have called us: to make You known and to glorify You, Father. For we pray and ask this in Jesus's name. Amen.

Questions for Reflection and Discussion

1. What two glaring leadership failures did Saul display in what he did following the attack on the Amalekites (see 15:9–21)?

2. What did Samuel say about God's view of obedience (see 15:22–23)?

Notes on Today's Bible Reading

— Day 8 —

Today's Reading: 1 Samuel 17

Verse of the Day

> And all the men of Israel, when they saw the man, fled from him and were dreadfully afraid.
>
> —*1 Samuel 17:24*

Please read the entire Scripture selection in your own Bible and highlight or underline verses that stand out to you before you read the observations and engage the questions below.

Today, our journey takes us to one of the most iconic chapters in all the Bible. Our key verse is 1 Samuel 17:24: "And all the men of Israel, when they saw the man, fled from him and were dreadfully afraid." However, also take note of 1 Samuel 17:48: "So it was, when the Philistine arose and came and drew near to meet David, that David hurried and ran toward the army to meet the Philistine." Those contrasting verses not only set the stage for our discussion, but they also present us with a decision. Confronted with a challenge, we will either be paralyzed by fear or propelled by faith. Keep that in mind as we explore the chapter for today.

We would be hard pressed to find someone who grew up in America who has not at least heard the phrase "David and Goliath." Certainly, every child who attended a church Bible school heard this well-known story. However, this is one of those biblical accounts we must approach with extra care because we have heard stories like this so many times that we are tempted to skim over it, thinking we already know what there is to know. When we do, we can miss some deeper truths that the Holy Spirit wants to teach us. Remember, God's Word is living and active. Consequently, slow down a bit here, look deeper into this encounter between David and Goliath, and ask the Holy Spirit to be your guide. As we examine this familiar story, some underlying principles found here are applicable to us today.

Before we begin with the text, allow me to offer some context. The Philistines likely got word of Saul's falling out of favor with Samuel, and they sought to take advantage of the situation. When there is a compromise of truth on the inside, there will be challenges on the outside. That is true of individuals. That is true of families. That is true of churches. That is true of nations. The enemy of our souls knows when we are vulnerable. With Saul engaged in this military standoff, he did not need David's services to play the harp to distract him from his tormenting spirit. So, David went back home to help his family, which apparently he did from time to time.

In 1 Samuel 17:8, we hear the taunt of Goliath: "Then he stood and cried out to the armies of Israel, and said to them, 'Why have you come out to line up for battle? Am I not a Philistine, and you the servants of Saul? Choose a man for yourselves, and let him come down to me.'" Now this may have been part of the army's problem. They allowed the enemy to define them as servants of Saul, and given Saul's character of compromise, there was little confidence among the men that God was with them. Skip ahead for a moment and consider how David describes the situation in 1 Samuel 17:45: "Then David said to the Philistine, 'You come to me with a sword, with a spear, and with a javelin. But I come to you in the name of the Lord of hosts, the God of the armies of Israel, whom you have defied.'" There is a big difference here in perspective. Our perspective on the challenges that we face and the power that we have, and where it comes from, really matters. Are we looking at the situation through the lens of what we can do, or are we looking through the lens of what God can do?

Back up to Goliath's continued taunting in 1 Samuel 17:10–11: "And the Philistine said, 'I defy the armies of Israel this day; give me a man, that we may fight together.' When Saul and all Israel heard these words of the Philistine, they were dismayed and greatly afraid." They were paralyzed by fear. What Goliath suggests was not unusual in ancient warfare among enemies that were well known to one another. Each army chose a combatant, a contestant, and they went out and fought, and the outcome determined what happened with the battle.

Look at 1 Samuel 17:15–16: "But David occasionally went and returned from Saul to feed his father's sheep at Bethlehem. And the Philistine drew near and presented himself forty days, morning and evening." Like a service member in the National Guard, David went back to the homefront to resume his responsibilities there with the flocks. Let us continue in 1 Samuel 17:17–18: "Then Jesse said to his son David, 'Take now for your brothers an ephah of this dried grain and these ten loaves, and run to your brothers at the camp. And carry these ten cheeses to the captain of their thousand, and see how your brothers fare, and bring back news of them.'" Apparently, this military stand-off had been going on for a while, and the family hadn't heard anything. Consequently, we read that Jesse sent David to the battle site: "So David rose early in the morning, left the sheep with a keeper, and took the things and went as Jesse had commanded him. And he came to the camp as the army was going out to the fight and shouting for the battle" (v. 20). This episode reveals David's humble character. Despite serving in the king's court, he went home to keep his father's sheep and obediently carry out his father's direction and help meet a need with the family. This is yet another reason David was a man after God's own heart. He had the heart of a humble servant.

When David arrived, he observed what was happening, and he asked some questions and he got some answers, along with some grief from his older brothers. We read in 1 Samuel 17:28, "Now Eliab his oldest brother heard when he spoke to the men; and Eliab's anger was aroused against David, and he said, 'Why did you come down here? And with whom have you left those few sheep in the wilderness? I know your pride and the insolence of your heart, for you have come down to see the battle.'" Please do not miss this. Eliab's criticism was more revealing of his own heart than the motives of David. He was projecting onto David what was most likely in Eliab's heart, which was pride and insolence. We must not allow the voices of the critics to discourage us from our duty to God. When we serve the Lord, we are going to have critics. Sometimes, our harshest critics will be the very people who are closest to us. However, we cannot allow the critics to discourage us from our duty.

We read that David was taken to Saul. David told him he was confident he could take out the giant because God had brought him through challenges and dangers before. Look at 1 Samuel 17:36: "'Your servant has killed both lion and bear; and this uncircumcised Philistine will be like one of them, seeing he has defied the armies of the living God.'" Some were saying this giant is too big to kill. David was saying he was too big to miss. Let us continue in 1 Samuel 17:37: "Moreover David said, 'The Lord, who delivered me from the paw of the lion and from the paw of the bear, He will deliver me from the hand of this Philistine.' And Saul said to David, 'Go, and the Lord be with you!'" I wonder how confident Saul was that David would be successful although he knew the past with God. It is important that we often reflect upon God's track record with us. The past with God is the foundation for future victories through God. This is true of nations. That is why we see repeatedly in the Old Testament they are recounting the history and what God did and how He showed up, oftentimes at the last minute. But He showed up.

Interestingly, Saul tried to get David to conform to his conventional notion of warfare: "So Saul clothed David with his armor, and he put a bronze helmet on his head; he also clothed him with a coat of mail. David fastened his sword to his armor and tried to walk, for he had not tested them. And David said to Saul, 'I cannot walk with these, for I have not tested them.' So David took them off" (vv. 38–39). That was the right move. For us, we should use what God has provided for us, not what He has given to someone else. Be who God has made you to be. Do not try to take someone else's talents and equipment. Try to do what He's called you to do and put in your heart.

There was something that rose up in David. Is there not a cause? And that is where we need to be, where the Holy Spirit leads us. We need to step out in faith. Look at 1 Samuel 17:40: "Then he took his staff in his hand; and he chose for himself five smooth stones from the brook, and put them in a shepherd's bag, in a pouch which he had, and his sling was in his hand. And he drew near to the Philistine." Again, David used the weapon he was equipped with, what he was familiar with, what he had trained to use, and he had been lethal with it. And he brought more to this epic battle than the simple weapon of a sling and a stone.

We read about it in 1 Samuel 17:45: "Then David said to the Philistine, 'You come to me with a sword, with a spear, and with a javelin. But I come to you in the name of the Lord of hosts, the God of the armies of Israel, whom you have defied.'" David made clear that this was the Lord's battle. Therefore, God would fight it: "'This day the Lord will deliver you into my hand, and I will strike you and take your head from you. And this day I will give the carcasses of the camp of the Philistines to the birds of the air and the wild beasts of the earth, that all the earth may know that there is a God in Israel. Then all this assembly shall know that the Lord does not save with sword and spear; for the battle is the Lord's, and He will give you into our hands'" (vv. 46–47).

What was this battle being fought over? David saw the bigger picture, the higher purpose: So that the world would know that God is in Israel and that He is the one who gives them the victory. It was all about God. Everything we do should be about bringing glory and honor to God.

Then we read about the clash of combatants in verses 48–49: "So it was, when the Philistine arose and came and drew near to meet David, that David hurried and ran toward the army to meet the Philistine. Then David put his hand in his bag and took out a stone; and he slung it and struck the Philistine in his forehead, so that the stone sank into his forehead, and he fell on his face to the earth." God gave young David the victory over the giant. We read about the result in 1 Samuel 17:51: "Therefore David ran and stood over the Philistine, took his sword and drew it out of its sheath and killed him, and cut off his head with it. And when the Philistines saw that their champion was dead, they fled." David took Goliath's sword, the sword intended to kill David, and he used it to kill the giant. God can take the instruments designed for use against us and turn them on our enemies. However, to get to that point, we have to step out in faith, use the skills we have been given to do what we can do, and trust God for what only He can do. This is a great account of David and Goliath, and so applicable to our lives today.

Prayer

Father, thank You for Your Word. Once again, Lord, we thank You for the Holy Spirit who is our teacher, leading us into all understanding of Your Word and how it applies to our lives. Lord, may we take these truths and may we use them, and may we bring honor and glory to You. Lord, for those who are facing some challenges, opposition, or spiritual battles that manifest themselves in different ways, relationships, work, or community, we pray they will know that these battles are Yours. May we give them to You because You fight these battles; You just want us to show up and step out in faith. So may we have that faith and may we be propelled by that faith. We pray in Jesus's name. Amen.

Questions for Reflection and Discussion

1. How did Saul and his army react to Goliath's challenge (see 17:11, 24)?
2. What can we learn from David's decision regarding Saul's armor (see 17:38–39)?

Notes on Today's Bible Reading

— Day 9 —

Today's Reading: 1 Samuel 18–19

Verse of the Day

> Now Saul was afraid of David, because the Lord was with him, but had departed from Saul.
>
> —*1 Samuel 18:12*

Please read the entire Scripture selection in your own Bible and highlight or underline verses that stand out to you before you read the observations and engage the questions below.

Our study brings us to 1 Samuel 18–19. Here is the question to consider: Is our confidence found in our position or in our posture? The contrast between David and Saul's posture and mindset will provide the right answer. The key verse is 1 Samuel 18:12: "Now Saul was afraid of David, because the Lord was with him, but had departed from Saul." It often strikes fear in the hearts of those who are opposed to God when they recognize the presence of God in their lives through what God is doing. Obviously, this does not mean that everything is perfect and problem-free. Saul opposed David. He tried to kill David, but God was with David, which was the defining issue.

We begin in 1 Samuel 18: "Now when he had finished speaking to Saul, the soul of Jonathan was knit to the soul of David, and Jonathan loved him as his own soul. Saul took him that day, and would not let him go home to his father's house anymore" (vv. 1–2). This chapter continues the storyline from chapter 17, where David killed Goliath. Continue in verses 3–4: "Then Jonathan and David made a covenant, because he loved him as his own soul. And Jonathan took off the robe that was on him and gave it to David, with his armor, even to his sword and his bow and his belt." As noted in our previous studies, Jonathan was King Saul's son and was in line, theoretically, to become king. However, he took off his royal robe and gave it to David.

Next, we read in verse 5, "So David went out wherever Saul sent him, and behaved wisely. And Saul set him over the men of war, and he was accepted in the sight of all the people and also in the sight of Saul's servants." Now, four times in this chapter we read that David behaved wisely. The meaning here is that he acted with prudence, and he prospered as a result. The Lord is the one who prospered and elevated him. Look at 1 Samuel 18:28a: "Thus Saul saw and knew that the LORD was with David." When we walk in the power of God's Holy Spirit by dwelling in His presence, as Jesus said, "He who abides in Me, and I in him, bears much fruit" (John 15:5b). David's conduct was such that God could prosper him, honor him, and elevate him in the kingdom.

Look at 1 Samuel 18:6–9:

> Now it had happened as they were coming home, when David was returning from the slaughter of the Philistine, that the women had come out of all the cities of Israel, singing and dancing, to meet King Saul, with tambourines, with joy, and with musical instruments. So the women sang as they danced, and said:
>
> "Saul has slain his thousands,
> And David his ten thousands."
>
> Then Saul was very angry, and the saying displeased him; and he said, "They have ascribed to David ten thousands, and to me they have ascribed only thousands. Now what more can

he have but the kingdom?" So Saul eyed David from that day forward.

Note the sharp contrast between David and Saul. David served selflessly, prospered by God, and David was successful in his military conquest against the Philistines. Though Saul was the one who benefited, he was consumed with the destructive forces of pride and jealousy. Pride and jealousy can blind us to reality and drive us to do dark things, which is what we see next in this account of David and Saul.

Read 1 Samuel 18:22–23: "And Saul commanded his servants, 'Communicate with David secretly, and say, "Look, the king has delight in you, and all his servants love you. Now therefore, become the king's son-in-law."' So, Saul's servants spoke those words in the hearing of David. And David said, 'Does it seem to you a light thing to be a king's son-in-law, seeing I am a poor and lightly esteemed man?'" Saul was scheming and trying to find a way to eliminate David. So, Saul decided to give David a chance to become his son-in-law by going on a dangerous and unnecessary military mission to kill one hundred Philistines. David humbly responded, "I am poor and lightly esteemed." This was his response despite the accolades given to him by all of those around him because of his military successes.

David's humility revealed that his confidence was not in his position but, rather, in his posture before God. The Spirit of God is the one who enabled David to act wisely and prudently, allowing God to prosper him. Recall 1 Samuel 16:13a, which says, "Then Samuel took the horn of oil and anointed him in the midst of his brothers; and the Spirit of the Lord came upon David from that day forward." Juxtapose David's posture of humility before the Lord, relying upon the power and the presence of the Holy Spirit, with that of Saul's position as king. Saul had the title, but he was one of the most insecure men whom we see in the Bible, afraid of his own shadow and under the stronghold of fear. If we abide in Christ, He does not give "us a spirit of fear, but of power and of love and of a sound mind" (2 Tim. 1:7).

Continue in 1 Samuel 18:28–29: "Thus Saul saw and knew that the LORD was with David, and that Michal, Saul's daughter, loved him; and Saul was still more afraid of David. So Saul became David's enemy continually." Despite Saul's clear animus toward him, David continued to behave wisely, and his name became highly esteemed. Saul, on the other hand, became more and more childish and foolish. David did his work as unto the Lord. He knew that he was serving the Lord ultimately, and that his reward would come from the Lord. Remember, it is possible to work for and with people who do not agree with our faith in the Lord. The world is becoming increasingly hostile to biblical truth and to God. It is important that believers respond as David did and not Saul. ("And whatever you do, do it heartily, as to the Lord and not to men, knowing that from the Lord you will receive the reward of the inheritance; for you serve the Lord Christ," Col. 3:23–24).

In 1 Samuel 19, Saul attempts to enlist others in his scheming and dirty work: "Now Saul spoke to Jonathan his son and to all his servants, that they should kill David; but Jonathan, Saul's son, delighted greatly in David. Jonathan told David, saying, 'My father Saul seeks to kill you. Therefore please be on your guard until morning, and stay in a secret place and hide'" (vv. 1–2). Jonathan, as we have seen before, was a man of character and conviction, unlike his father. He not only risked incurring his father's wrath by foiling Saul's plan to kill David, but Jonathan's actions ensured that he would not be king after his father. The throne was going to David. What a contrast. Saul would kill to keep the throne. Jonathan would die to lose the throne to ensure that the man whom God had chosen succeeded. Please do not miss that point. Jonathan understood God's plan for the kingdom, for David, and for himself. He was not driven by aspirations to succeed in the eyes of the world but to embrace God's call on his life. His call was to be second, to serve the one whom God was elevating to lead.

Continue in 1 Samuel 19:4–7:

> Thus Jonathan spoke well of David to Saul his father, and said to him, "Let not the king sin against his servant, against David, because he has not sinned against you, and because his works have been very good toward you. For he took his life in his hands and killed the Philistine, and the LORD brought about a great deliverance for all Israel. You saw it and rejoiced. Why then will you sin against innocent blood, to kill David without a cause?" So Saul heeded the voice of Jonathan, and Saul swore, "As the LORD lives, he shall not be killed." Then Jonathan called David, and Jonathan told him all these things. So Jonathan brought David to Saul, and he was in his presence as in times past.

Jonathan prevailed in talking sense into his father, but it did not last long.

In 1 Samuel 19:8, we read more of David's exploits as a warrior: "And there was war again; and David went out and fought with the Philistines, and struck them with a mighty blow, and they fled from him." David's continued success on the battlefield doubtless fueled Saul's jealousy: "Now the distressing spirit from the LORD came upon Saul as he sat in his house with his spear in his hand. And David was playing music with his hand" (v. 9). Saul was in his own home with his security around him. Why does he have a spear in his hand when David was playing music with his hand? Here is yet another difference between these two men: Saul had a weapon of destruction in his hand, while David had an instrument of worship in his. In a jealous rage, Saul tries to kill David: "Then Saul sought to pin David to the wall with the spear, but he slipped away from Saul's presence; and he drove the spear into the wall. So David fled and escaped that night" (v. 10). David then went to Samuel, and he stayed among the prophets. Saul, however, was undeterred and was hot on his trail. He sent messengers to get him and bring him back so he could kill him.

Drop down to 1 Samuel 19:20–24:

> Then Saul sent messengers to take David. And when they saw the group of prophets prophesying, and Samuel standing as leader over them, the Spirit of God came upon the messengers of Saul, and they also prophesied. And when Saul was told, he sent other messengers, and they prophesied likewise. Then Saul sent messengers again the third time, and they prophesied also. Then he also went to Ramah, and came to the great well that is at Sechu. So he asked, and said, "Where are Samuel and David?" And someone said, "Indeed they are at Naioth in Ramah." So he went there to Naioth in Ramah. Then the Spirit of God was upon him also, and he went on and prophesied until he came to Naioth in Ramah. And he also stripped off his clothes and prophesied before Samuel in like manner, and lay down naked all that day and all that night. Therefore they say, "Is Saul also among the prophets?"

This account requires some explanation. Was Saul among the prophets? It was clear that he was among them but not one of them. God spoke through Balaam's donkey, so God can speak through and use other instruments as well. There is no evidence at all that Saul's heart was changed, but the power of God overcame Saul, resulting in him stripping off the vestiges of power and pride and being humbled before God and God's servants.

Prayer

Father, we thank You for Your Word. And Lord, help us to find our strength not in our position or in our title but in our posture before

You, abiding in the Lord Jesus Christ. For there is where we find our strength, our encouragement, our hope. That is where we are able to bear fruit in our lives so that others will take note—even those who may be unsettled by the presence of God. But we pray, through our testimony and witness in our faithfulness to You, that others will be drawn toward You. We continue to ask for the Holy Spirit to guide us on our journey through Your Word. Father, those who are struggling right now with people who oppose them for no reason—whether it is in a position, a job, or somewhere else—we pray for breakthroughs and that they will continue to be faithful in following You. And Lord, that You will elevate them and honor them as they abide in You. In Jesus's name. Amen.

Questions for Reflection and Discussion

1. What prompted Saul to eye David with suspicion and jealousy (see 18:7–9)?

2. What happened to the men Saul sent to Naioth to capture David (see 19:20–24)?

Notes on Today's Bible Reading

— Day 10 —

Today's Reading: 1 Samuel 20–21

Verse of the Day

> "Have I need of madmen, that you have brought this fellow to play the madman in my presence? Shall this fellow come into my house?"
>
> —*1 Samuel 21:15*

Please read the entire Scripture selection in your own Bible and highlight or underline verses that stand out to you before you read the observations and engage the questions below

---

Our study finds us in 1 Samuel 20–21, and our key verse is 1 Samuel 21:15: "'Have I need of madmen, that you have brought this fellow to play the madman in my presence? Shall this fellow come into my house?'" From here to the end of the book of 1 Samuel, it is clear that Saul's heart is hardened, while David's heart is still pliable as it is tested and shaped through adversity.

Start in 1 Samuel 20:1–5:

> Then David fled from Naioth in Ramah, and went and said to Jonathan, "What have I done? What is my iniquity, and what is my sin before your father, that he seeks my life?" Jonathan said to him, "By no means! You shall not die! Indeed, my father will do nothing either great or small without first telling me. And why should my father hide this thing from me? It is not so!" Then David took an oath again, and said,

> "Your father certainly knows that I have found favor in your eyes, and he has said, 'Do not let Jonathan know this, lest he be grieved.' But truly, as the LORD lives and as your soul lives, there is but a step between me and death." So Jonathan said to David, "Whatever you yourself desire, I will do it for you." And David said to Jonathan, "Indeed tomorrow is the New Moon, and I should not fail to sit with the king to eat. But let me go, that I may hide in the field until the third day at evening."

The beginning of the new month, or new moon, was always celebrated with a special sacrifice and followed by feasting. All the family members were expected to be present for these occasions, which were both spiritual and civil celebrations. David went knowing that he was just one step from the grave, basically because Saul was in hot pursuit.

Continue in 1 Samuel 20:6–7: "'If your father misses me at all, then say, "David earnestly asked permission of me that he might run over to Bethlehem, his city, for there is a yearly sacrifice there for all the family." If he says thus: "It is well," your servant will be safe. But if he is very angry, be sure that evil is determined by him.'" They discussed where David would be waiting for the answer and how they would communicate to each other once Jonathan had a reading on his father. Thus, David did not show up for the first night of the meal. Nothing was said.

On the second night. Saul asked why David was not present.

> So Jonathan answered Saul, "David earnestly asked permission of me to go to Bethlehem. And he said, 'Please let me go, for our family has a sacrifice in the city, and my brother has commanded me to be there. And now, if I have found favor in your eyes, please let me get away and see my brothers.' Therefore he has not come to the king's table." Then Saul's anger

> was aroused against Jonathan, and he said to him, "You son of a perverse, rebellious woman! Do I not know that you have chosen the son of Jesse to your own shame and to the shame of your mother's nakedness?" (vv. 28–30)

This was an epic insult. It was as if he was saying, "It would have been better that you had never been born. It was a shame for your mother to give birth to you." First Samuel 20:31 says, "'For as long as the son of Jesse lives on the earth, you shall not be established, nor your kingdom. Now therefore, send and bring him to me, for he shall surely die.'" David had his answer and was not good at concealing the intent of his heart. As Jesus said in Matthew 12:34b, "'For out of the abundance of the heart the mouth speaks.'" What is said, especially in moments of anger, reveals what is in the heart. Frankly, that is a good time to stop and take spiritual inventory. When anger erupts like a volcano and destructive words are spoken, it is not enough to have remorse and say, "I am sorry for the words that I have spoken." This is a heart issue revealed that needs to be rectified. Saul never did that.

David and Jonathan then meet for what appeared to be the last time. After becoming a fugitive, David fled to Nob, the place of the priests were located. Nob had taken the place of Shiloh after the capture of the ark of the covenant. Look at 1 Samuel 21:1–3:

> Now David came to Nob, to Ahimelech the priest. And Ahimelech was afraid when he met David, and said to him, "Why are you alone, and no one is with you?" David said to Ahimelech the priest, "The king has ordered me on some business, and said to me, 'Do not let anyone know anything about the business on which I send you, or what I have commanded you.' And I have directed my young men to such and such a place. Now therefore, what have you on hand? Give me five loaves of bread in my hand, or whatever can be found."

This is one of those recorded accounts of David in which he acted out of character with someone who is after God's own heart. Here, David lied. And his lie, as we will see in chapter 22, cost the lives of many innocent people.

He then asked about a sword in 1 Samuel 21:8–9, "And David said to Ahimelech, 'Is there not here on hand a spear or a sword? For I have brought neither my sword nor my weapons with me, because the king's business required haste.' So the priest said, 'The sword of Goliath the Philistine, whom you killed in the Valley of Elah, there it is, wrapped in a cloth behind the ephod. If you will take that, take it. For there is no other except that one here.' And David said, 'There is none like it; give it to me.'" David reclaimed the sword of Goliath, which had been placed with the priest, apparently in the tabernacle, or what was serving as a tabernacle at the time.

Next we read in 1 Samuel 21:10, "Then David arose and fled that day from before Saul, and went to Achish the king of Gath." Now, does Gath sound vaguely familiar? That was the home of Goliath. So, David was going to the home of the giant that he killed carrying the giant's sword. There was none like it. It was quite identifiable. It would appear that David was not trusting in the Lord, but out of fear, being shaken by the unjustified and unfair circumstances that he was facing, he acted in his own wisdom, which was lacking.

Now it is possible that Achish was someone with whom David had favor. It could be that Goliath was actually a political problem for Achish, and David did him a favor by killing him. David went to Gath assuming Achish would protect him because he was now an enemy of Saul. Perhaps David was relying on the old adage, "The enemy of my enemy is my friend." However, the people of Gath began to ask questions.

Look at 1 Samuel 21:11–12: "And the servants of Achish said to him, 'Is this not David the king of the land? Did they not sing of him to one another in dances, saying: "Saul has slain his thousands and David his ten thousands"?' Now David took these words to heart, and was very much afraid of Achish the king of Gath." Maybe David started coming to his senses, or fear was gripping him. Once fear takes over, it usually consumes and lurks around every corner. That is why Scripture states in 2 Timothy 1:7, "God has not given us a spirit of fear, but of power and of love and of sound mind." Unfortunately, fear continued to creep in David's heart.

Consequently, David puts on a show as we read in 1 Samuel 21:13: "So he changed his behavior before them, pretended madness in their hands, scratched on the doors of the gate, and let his saliva fall down on his beard." He was acting like a crazy man. David realized that Achish had a political problem of his own, and Gath would not be a safe haven for him, so he acted crazy so he could get out. David trusted in himself and others, which left him acting like a crazy man. In Psalm 118:8-9, David apparently learned his lesson at some point: "It is better to trust in the Lord than to put confidence in man. It is better to trust in the Lord than to put confidence in princes." How true that is.

Prayer

Father, we pray that we will put our confidence and our trust in You and that, Lord, we will not operate out of fear, even when we face unfair circumstances, unjustified circumstances, and threats. But, Lord, it is in those moments that we need to trust You and not act in our own wisdom because often the decisions we make in those moments not only affect our lives but the lives of others. So, Father, give us through the Holy Spirit that confidence, that power, that sound mind, that love. Lord, we pray the Holy Spirit will continue to guide us on this journey, that we might know how to rightfully apply Your Word to our lives this day. In Jesus's name. Amen.

Questions for Reflection and Discussion

1. When Jonathan told the lad, "the arrows are beyond you," what was he communicating to David (see 20:22, 36–39)?

2. What did David do in Gath when he became afraid that Achish might take revenge on him (see 21:12–14)?

Notes on Today's Bible Reading

— Day 11 —

Today's Reading: 1 Samuel 22–23

Verse of the Day

> And David stayed in strongholds in the wilderness, and remained in the mountains in the Wilderness of Ziph. Saul sought him every day, but God did not deliver him into his hand.
>
> *—1 Samuel 23:14*

Please read the entire Scripture selection in your own Bible and highlight or underline verses that stand out to you before you read the observations and engage the questions below

---

A new chapter in the life of David begins in 1 Samuel 22–23. The key verse is 1 Samuel 23:14: "And David stayed in strongholds in the wilderness, and remained in the mountains in the Wilderness of Ziph. Saul sought him every day, but God did not deliver him into his hand." David began to assemble his core leadership team, some of whom would remain with him for the rest of his life. God was preparing David to lead through difficulty and adversity. God uses challenges and often distressing events in our lives to prepare us for greater service. Such was the case with David.

First Samuel 22:1 states, "David therefore departed from there and escaped to the cave of Adullam. So when his brothers and all his father's house heard it, they went down there to him." This seems to be evidence of God's anointing on David. Recall when Saul was anointed in chapter 10: "and valiant men went with him, whose hearts God had touched" (v. 26b). The anointing of God will attract people. Leaders sometimes make the mistake of thinking it is all about them, when in fact it is the power of God upon them.

At this point, David was essentially enrolled in an intensive course in leadership. An eclectic group was attracted to him: "And everyone who was in distress, everyone who was in debt, and everyone who was discontented gathered to him. So he became captain over them. And there were about four hundred men with him" (1 Sam. 22:2). In many ways, this had to be an extremely difficult group to lead. Yet, if David could master leading this group, he would be prepared to lead the nation.

Continue in 1 Samuel 22:3–4: "Then David went from there to Mizpah of Moab; and he said to the king of Moab, 'Please let my father and mother come here with you, till I know what God will do for me.' So he brought them before the king of Moab, and they dwelt with him all the time that David was in the stronghold." There was concern for the safety of his parents. David took them to Moab, the land of his great-grandmother Ruth. He understood how evil and despotic Saul was, and he did not want his parents to be used as leverage against him or for them to be harmed.

Look at 1 Samuel 22:5: "Now the prophet Gad said to David, 'Do not stay in the stronghold; depart, and go to the land of Judah.' So David departed and went into the forest of Hereth." Now I do not know the significance of this specific instruction from Gad, why they were to go to this particular place, but I do believe the significance here is this shows another contrast between David and Saul. David listened to and acted upon the instruction of the prophets of God. This is where again we see a separation between David and Saul.

Next we read that Saul stirred up his tribe against David in 1 Samuel 22:7–8:

> [T]hen Saul said to his servants who stood about him, "Hear now, you Benjamites! Will the son of Jesse give every one of

> you fields and vineyards, and make you all captains of thousands and captains of hundreds? All of you have conspired against me, and there is no one who reveals to me that my son has made a covenant with the son of Jesse; and there is not one of you who is sorry for me or reveals to me that my son has stirred up my servant against me, to lie in wait, as it is this day."

This is extremely revealing of the self-centered nature of Saul. As these next chapters lay out, Saul was consumed with trying to kill David. He accused the men around him of being bribed by David to betray Saul. He accused his son of treason, and he said of David, who was running for his life from Saul's murderous plot, that he was an insurrectionist. Saul believed that everyone was against him.

Next, he accused Ahimelech the priest of siding with David because of the bread and sword he gave to David when he thought David was on a mission for the king. Look at 1 Samuel 22:13–16:

> Then Saul said to him, "Why have you conspired against me, you and the son of Jesse, in that you have given him bread and a sword, and have inquired of God for him, that he should rise against me, to lie in wait, as it is this day?" So Ahimelech answered the king and said, "And who among all your servants is as faithful as David, who is the king's son-in-law, who goes at your bidding, and is honorable in your house? Did I then begin to inquire of God for him? Far be it from me! Let not the king impute anything to his servant, or to any in the house of my father. For your servant knew nothing of all this, little or much." And the king said, "You shall surely die, Ahimelech, you and all your father's house!"

So, in contrast to David, who listened to the words of the men of God, Saul had them killed, accusing them of treason.

We read of the tragic result in 1 Samuel 22:17–19:

> Then the king said to the guards who stood about him, "Turn and kill the priests of the LORD, because their hand also is with David, and because they knew when he fled and did not tell it to me." But the servants of the king would not lift their hands to strike the priests of the LORD. And the king said to Doeg, "You turn and kill the priests!" So Doeg the Edomite turned and struck the priests, and killed on that day eighty-five men who wore a linen ephod. Also Nob, the city of the priests, he struck with the edge of the sword, both men and women, children and nursing infants, oxen and donkeys and sheep—with the edge of the sword.

This was both brutal and godless. That describes Saul and his accomplices. Continue in 1 Samuel 22:20–23: "Now one of the sons of Ahimelech the son of Ahitub, named Abiathar, escaped and fled after David. And Abiathar told David that Saul had killed the LORD's priests. So David said to Abiathar, 'I knew that day, when Doeg the Edomite was there, that he would surely tell Saul. I have caused the death of all the persons of your father's house. Stay with me; do not fear. For he who seeks my life seeks your life, but with me you shall be safe.'" So, here David took responsibility for the lie he told that led to the deaths of these innocent people. It was a travesty. David, though he was a man after God's own heart, stepped outside the hands of God and put them into his hands, which led to tragic consequences. This is a lesson to be learned by all believers.

Next we read in 1 Samuel 23:1–2, "Then they told David, saying, 'Look, the Philistines are fighting against Keilah, and they are robbing the threshing floors.' Therefore David inquired of the LORD, saying, 'Shall I go and attack these Philistines?' And the LORD said to David, 'Go and attack the Philistines, and save Keilah.'" Notice what was happening here. David had no position in Saul's army or title in the government of Israel. Yet he served in the Lord's army and was commissioned by God. Believers have the authority to operate and seek direction from the Lord and operate in that authority in obedience to God, as David did here. Out of compassion and a sense of duty, he went to the aid of these beleaguered Israelites.

Yet his leadership was questioned by his men as we see in 1 Samuel 22:3: "But David's men said to him, 'Look, we are afraid here in Judah. How much more then if we go to Keilah against the armies of the Philistines?'" Frankly, this too was a part of the leadership training. David had to bring his men along, which is the task of a leader: "Then David inquired of the LORD once again. And the LORD answered him and said, 'Arise, go down to Keilah. For I will deliver the Philistines into your hand.' And David and his men went to Keilah and fought with the Philistines, struck them with a mighty blow, and took away their livestock. So David saved the inhabitants of Keilah" (vv. 4–5). Nothing solidifies a team like a great victory in the face of overwhelming odds.

Read on in 1 Samuel 23:7: "And Saul was told that David had gone to Keilah. So Saul said, 'God has delivered him into my hand, for he has shut himself in by entering a town that has gates and bars.'" Saul received intelligence that David was in a vulnerable position, heard where he was, and wanted to try to kill him—yet another stark contrast between the two of them. David sought direction from the Lord, while Saul falsely credited God with assisting his own evil desire to kill David. Saul attempted to use the name of God in a pretense of spirituality to advance his godless agenda. This reminds me of what Jesus said to His disciples in John 16:2: "'They will put you out of the synagogues; yes, the time is coming that whoever kills you will think that he offers God service.'"

By contrast, David did not presume on God's will, He inquired of the Lord. Look at 1 Samuel 23:11–13: "'Will the men of Keilah deliver me into his hand? Will Saul come down, as Your servant has heard? O Lord God of Israel, I pray, tell Your servant.' And the Lord said, 'He will come down.' Then David said, 'Will the men of Keilah deliver me and my men into the hand of Saul?' And the Lord said, 'They will deliver you.' So David and his men, about six hundred, arose and departed from Keilah and went wherever they could go. Then it was told Saul that David had escaped from Keilah; so he halted the expedition." Notice that David's band of men was growing. It was four hundred previously. At this point, it has grown to six hundred.

We read in 1 Samuel 23:14: "And David stayed in strongholds in the wilderness, and remained in the mountains in the Wilderness of Ziph. Saul sought him every day, but God did not deliver him into his hand." Now, Saul was obsessed with pursuing David every day. The kingdom had to be crumbling. The roads, drainage, all of the things that government should be doing were not being taken care of because Saul was obsessed with his political opponent.

Let us continue in verses 15–16: "So David saw that Saul had come out to seek his life. And David was in the Wilderness of Ziph in a forest. Then Jonathan, Saul's son, arose and went to David in the woods and strengthened his hand in God." Notice that Saul couldn't find him, but Jonathan knew where to find David. In fact, this was the final meeting between Jonathan and David. Once again, Jonathan pledged his support to David and embraced God's plan for David's life. We read in 1 Samuel 23:17, "And he said to him, 'Do not fear, for the hand of Saul my father shall not find you. You shall be king over Israel, and I shall be next to you. Even my father Saul knows that.'" Again, note the selflessness of Jonathan. He too provided such a contrast with his father. We read in verse 18, "So the two of them made a covenant before the Lord. And David stayed in the woods, and Jonathan went to his own house."

Near the end of the chapter we find yet another example of how Saul tried to "sanctify" his own sin. The Ziphites sent word to Saul that they knew where David was hiding, obviously attempting to gain favor with the maniacal king. We read in 1 Samuel 23:20–21, "'Now therefore, O king, come down according to all the desire of your soul to come down; and our part shall be to deliver him into the king's hand.' And Saul said, 'Blessed are you of the LORD, for you have compassion on me.'" Again, look at the self-centered nature where Saul declared people being "blessed" because they were favorable toward him. How can anyone be blessed by the Lord when they are working against the Lord? Yet Saul, consumed with himself, considered everyone who did anything favorable toward him "blessed of the LORD." He was not aware or refused to acknowledge that God had departed from him. Strength, power, and blessing of the Lord comes by walking in obedience and submission to the Lord. Saul was not walking in that manner. His negative example should challenge us to walk otherwise.

Prayer

Father, thank You for Your Word. And again, we just thank You for the tremendous understanding that is found in the contrast between these two men, Saul and David. May our hearts be devoted to You, Lord, that we will walk in total and absolute obedience to You, bringing glory and honor to Your name. Again, we thank You for Your Word, and we pray this in Jesus's name. Amen.

Questions for Reflection and Discussion

1. What kind of men joined David at the cave of Adullam (see 22:1–2)?
   a. Successful
   b. Prosperous
   c. Desperate
   d. All the above

2. Saul sought David every day, but why could he not find him (see 23:14)?

Notes on Today's Bible Reading

— Day 12 —

Today's Reading: 1 Samuel 24–25

Verse of the Day

> "Therefore let the LORD be judge, and judge between you and me, and see and plead my case, and deliver me out of your hand."
>
> —*1 Samuel 24:15*

Please read the entire Scripture selection in your own Bible and highlight or underline verses that stand out to you before you read the observations and engage the questions below.

Today we are going to look at the difference between using the Lord and listening to the Lord. Our key verse is from 1 Samuel 24:15: "'Therefore let the LORD be judge, and judge between you and me, and see and plead my case, and deliver me out of your hand.'" We find yet another contrast between Saul and David in 1 Samuel 24–25.

In chapter 24, David is on the run. He is a fugitive. He has become the leader of a growing group of those in distress and discontent. He was hiding down in the rugged wilderness of En Gedi. Once again, Saul received intelligence of his location. Consequently, Saul gathered his army in pursuit of David:

> Then Saul took three thousand chosen men from all Israel, and went to seek David and his men on the Rocks of the Wild

> Goats. So he came to the sheepfolds by the road, where there was a cave; and Saul went in to attend to his needs. (David and his men were staying in the recesses of the cave.) Then the men of David said to him, "This is the day of which the LORD said to you, 'Behold, I will deliver your enemy into your hand, that you may do to him as it seems good to you.'" And David arose and secretly cut off a corner of Saul's robe. Now it happened afterward that David's heart troubled him because he had cut Saul's robe. And he said to his men, "The LORD forbid that I should do this thing to my master, the LORD's anointed, to stretch out my hand against him, seeing he is the anointed of the LORD." So David restrained his servants with these words, and did not allow them to rise against Saul. And Saul got up from the cave and went on his way. (vv. 2–7)

To whom was David listening? He was not listening to his men who said, basically, "Hey, this is your chance. Take him out. The Lord has delivered your enemy into your hands." But David did not listen to them. He was listening to the Lord.

Think about this. Saul used the Lord to justify his wicked and evil plans. David, on the other hand, listened to the Lord and restrained his hand from evil. He did not use the Lord to justify what he was doing. David listened to the Lord to keep him from doing what he should not. Believers cannot stop listening to the Lord and His Word. Remember what Samuel told Saul back in 1 Samuel 15 when he did what he wanted to do? Saul did not listen to God. Samuel said, "'You have rejected the word of the LORD, and the LORD has rejected you'" (v. 26b). When we stop listening to the Lord, that is when we get off and we begin to justify evil in the name of the Lord.

Then 1 Samuel 24:8–10 relates,

> David also arose afterward, went out of the cave, and called out to Saul, saying, "My lord the king!" And when Saul looked behind him, David stooped with his face to the earth, and bowed down. And David said to Saul: "Why do you listen to the words of men who say, 'Indeed David seeks your harm'? Look, this day your eyes have seen that the LORD delivered you today into my hand in the cave, and someone urged me to kill you. But my eye spared you, and I said, 'I will not stretch out my hand against my lord, for he is the LORD's anointed.'"

Let us go to verse 12, "'Let the LORD judge between you and me, and let the LORD avenge me on you. But my hand shall not be against you.'" Here is an extremely important lesson, applicable to each of us. David trusted in the Lord to avenge him against those who would do evil to him. In the next chapter, he almost blew it by trying to avenge himself. But fortunately, another wise and industrious woman leaps off the pages of Scripture to save the day. It is tempting, but believers cannot listen to the voices of even trusted friends. The word and voice of the Lord must be the only one heard, and He will work out the trials and temptations in life.

Let us continue in 1 Samuel 24:13–19"

> "As the proverb of the ancients says, 'Wickedness proceeds from the wicked.' But my hand shall not be against you. After whom has the king of Israel come out? Whom do you pursue? A dead dog? A flea? Therefore let the LORD be judge, and judge between you and me, and see and plead my case, and deliver me out of your hand." So it was, when David had finished speaking these words to Saul, that Saul said, "Is this your voice, my son David?" And Saul lifted up his voice and wept. Then he said to David: "You are more righteous than I; for you

> have rewarded me with good, whereas I have rewarded you with evil. And you have shown this day how you have dealt well with me; for when the LORD delivered me into your hand, you did not kill me. For if a man finds his enemy, will he let him get away safely? Therefore may the LORD reward you with good for what you have done to me this day."

This was a rare and passing moment of remorse and sanity for Saul, where his hatred and jealousy of David was eclipsed.

Continue in verses 20–22: "And now I know indeed that you shall surely be king, and that the kingdom of Israel shall be established in your hand. Therefore swear now to me by the LORD that you will not cut off my descendants after me, and that you will not destroy my name from my father's house. So David swore to Saul. And Saul went home, but David and his men went to the stronghold." David had seen this before. He knew better than to go back with Saul because it would be only a matter of time before Saul became hostile and go after him again.

Chapter 25 begins with the death of Samuel, the prophet, priest, and judge as well as David's mentor. Then there is an account of David's "private protection agency" in action. They were protecting the people from the raiders and doing what Saul really should have been doing had he not been so preoccupied with chasing David. However, this also builds goodwill between David and the people as we will see later.

Specifically, David protected the servants and the flocks of a wealthy man named Nabal. Yet when David asked for a little renumeration for the services that he had provided, Nabal rebuffs David and his men. David does not respond well on this occasion. Enraged, David prepares to massacre Nabal's entire household. However, Nabal's wise wife, Abigail, quickly intervenes. Without telling her husband, she prepares a large gift of food and meets

David on the road. With deep humility, she pleads for David to consider his future as king, urging him not to stain his legacy with unnecessary bloodshed. David relents, recognizing God's hand in Abigail's counsel.

Had Abigail not interceded with David, and he not received it, the outcome would have been bad. Thankfully, David's greatness shone through his humility in listening to Abigail, a woman he didn't know. True wisdom is being willing to receive correction from anyone God chooses to send. Shortly after, Nabal dies after hearing of the close encounter, an event the text attributes to divine judgment. Not surprisingly, his name literally means "fool." David then takes Abigail as his wife. Chapter 25 is another tremendous account of an amazing woman used by God to save the day.

Prayer

Father, we thank You for Your Word and for the examples of godly verses selfish responses found in the lives of David and Saul. Father, help us listen to You and not use Your name to justify our own evil desires. May our hearts be pure before You. And we pray the Holy Spirit will lead us in applying Your Word to our lives and to the world in which we live. Thank You. In Jesus name, amen.

Questions for Reflection and Discussion

1. What did David's men suggest God was doing when Saul came into the cave where they were hiding (see 24:4)?

2. What did Abigail's wise appeal keep David from doing (see 25:31–34)?

Notes on Today's Bible Reading

— Day 13 —

Today's Reading: 1 Samuel 26–28

Verse of the Day

> And David said in his heart, "Now I shall perish someday by the hand of Saul. There is nothing better for me than that I should speedily escape to the land of the Philistines."
>
> *—1 Samuel 27:1a*

Please read the entire Scripture selection in your own Bible and highlight or underline verses that stand out to you before you read the observations and engage the questions below.

Today we are examining 1 Samuel 26–28. Our key verse is 1 Samuel 27:1a, "And David said in his heart, 'Now I shall perish someday by the hand of Saul. There is nothing better for me than that I should speedily escape to the land of the Philistines.'" Where does your hope and your help come from now? Later, David wrote,

> I will lift up my eyes to the hills—
> From whence comes my help?
> My help comes from the Lord,
> Who made heaven and earth. (Ps. 121:1–2)

The reason David wrote that psalm is the subject of some debate, but we will see in today's passage that this declaration David made has life application for all of us.

In 1 Samuel 26, David and his men were in the wilderness of Ziph. Once again, despite his previous declarations of remorse, Saul was on a search-and-destroy mission. An insecure heart walled off from God, inflamed by jealousy, is not only irrational but also predictably dangerous. That is Saul.

Let us start in 1 Samuel 26:4–9:

> David therefore sent out spies, and understood that Saul had indeed come. So David arose and came to the place where Saul had encamped. And David saw the place where Saul lay, and Abner the son of Ner, the commander of his army. Now Saul lay within the camp, with the people encamped all around him. Then David answered, and said to Ahimelech the Hittite and to Abishai the son of Zeruiah, brother of Joab, saying, "Who will go down with me to Saul in the camp?" And Abishai said, "I will go down with you." So David and Abishai came to the people by night; and there Saul lay sleeping within the camp, with his spear stuck in the ground by his head. And Abner and the people lay all around him. Then Abishai said to David, "God has delivered your enemy into your hand this day. Now therefore, please, let me strike him at once with the spear, right to the earth; and I will not have to strike him a second time!" But David said to Abishai, "Do not destroy him; for who can stretch out his hand against the LORD's anointed, and be guiltless?"

This is the second recorded occurrence in which David was encouraged to kill Saul by those around him. They urged him with the same message: "God has delivered your enemy into your hand." They were saying, "This is twice the LORD has delivered him into your hands." However, David knew that was contrary to God's Word. Unlike Saul, David refused to conform the Word of God to his circumstances. Rather, he conformed his behavior to the Word of God. This tendency to conform to the world is common among those who are not abiding in Christ. Romans 12:2 says, "And do not be conformed to this world, but be transformed by the renewing of your mind, that you may prove what is that good and acceptable and perfect will of God." God beckons us to renew our mind daily in His Holy Word.

Let us continue in 1 Samuel 26:10–12:

> David said furthermore, "As the LORD lives, the LORD shall strike him, or his day shall come to die, or he shall go out to battle and perish. The LORD forbid that I should stretch out my hand against the LORD's anointed. But please, take now the spear and the jug of water that are by his head, and let us go." So David took the spear and the jug of water by Saul's head, and they got away; and no man saw or knew it or awoke. For they were all asleep, because a deep sleep from the LORD had fallen on them."

Here, we see God's hand directly in the affairs of man. A deep sleep was upon the camp so that David and Abishai could walk in and out. Then David went to a hilltop a good distance away, and he yelled back to Abner, who was the head of Saul's military and should have been protecting him.

Look at 1 Samuel 26:16: "'This thing that you have done is not good. As the LORD lives, you deserve to die, because you have not guarded your master, the LORD's anointed. And now see where the king's spear is, and the jug of water that was by his head.'" Remember last time he cut off the corner of his garment? Then verse 17: "Saul knew David's voice, and said, 'Is that your voice, my son David?' David said, 'It is my voice, my lord, O king.'" Then skip down to verse 21: "Then Saul said, 'I have sinned. Return, my son David. For I will harm you no more, because my life was precious in your eyes this day. Indeed I have played the fool and erred exceedingly.'" David had heard that before, and he knew that he could not count on Saul to keep his word. After all, he did not keep his word to God. Consequently, David knew he was not safe in the hands of Saul. Here we see the application of David's declaration in Psalm 121. David looked to the Lord for help, to be the one who repays us for what we do, whether good or bad. We do not look to man. We do not look to the hills for reinforcements. We look to the One who made heaven and earth.

Continue in 1 Samuel 26:23–24: "'May the LORD repay every man for his righteousness and his faithfulness; for the LORD delivered you into my hand today, but I would not stretch out my hand against the LORD's anointed. And indeed, as your life was valued much this day in my eyes, so let my life be valued much in the eyes of the LORD, and let Him deliver me out of all tribulation.'" We cannot apply one standard to our behavior and a different standard to others. It is a universal standard. Values and morals are not selective, nor are they relative to our feelings. We do not determine what they are. They are universal, fixed by God.

In chapter 27, David listened to his own thoughts and not the voice of the Lord. Unfortunately, we just had this great victory, then David moved away from God's declared plan into the idolatrous land of Israel's avowed enemy, Philistia. This area has always been a problem and encompasses the modern-day Gaza strip. It has long been a spiritual stronghold for evil. The situation was different this time than the previous. He was welcomed by the king of Gath, Achish. It could be that the split between Saul and David was widely known, so there was no fear that David's defection would be a plot. So, David and his men were given the area of Ziklag as their base of operations. These were the areas David attacked and destroyed, and, in fact, the areas that God originally said should be cleaned out. However, David was less than honest with Achish.

Read 1 Samuel 27:10–12:

> Then Achish would say, "Where have you made a raid today?" And David would say, "Against the southern area of Judah, or against the southern area of the Jerahmeelites, or against the southern area of the Kenites." David would save neither man nor woman alive, to bring news to Gath, saying, "Lest they should inform on us, saying, 'Thus David did.'" And thus was his behavior all the time he dwelt in the country of the Philistines. So Achish believed David, saying, "He has made his people Israel utterly abhor him; therefore he will be my servant forever."

The question is: Is this dishonest? Is it wrong? We see accounts in Scripture, like with the midwives back in Exodus who were not honest with Pharaoh, so that lives could be saved. Some would say this is a violation of one of the Ten Commandments, which says we are not to bear false witness, not to falsely state something against someone else. And many have wrestled with this passage over the millennia, and there are no easy answers.

Chapter 28 begins with Achish summoning David for a pending war with Israel and ends with an odd account of Saul and the witch of En Dor. Let us look at 1 Samuel 28:5: "When Saul saw the army of the Philistines, he was afraid, and his heart trembled greatly." What a miserable person Saul must have been, living in fear of everything. Honestly, this is the state of people when they are alienated from God. He was afraid David was going to take the kingdom. He was afraid of the enemy. When we are alienated from God, there is no confidence because we are not standing on anything firm. The very ground beneath his feet was unstable—he had no foundation.

Continue in 1 Samuel 28:6–7: "And when Saul inquired of the LORD, the LORD did not answer him, either by dreams or by Urim or by the prophets. Then Saul said to his servants, 'Find me a woman who is a medium, that I may go to her and inquire of her.' And his servants said to him, 'In fact, there is a woman who is a medium at En Dor.'" Remember, it was Saul who rejected the Word of the Lord, so the Lord rejected him. That is why Saul received no answer. As pointed out previously, the Lord speaks to us through His Word. If we repeatedly and habitually ignore that Word by not reading it or by not heeding it, then we cannot expect God to continue to speak to us, nor to communicate to us in other ways. If we are not listening, if we are not obeying, God is going to quit speaking. If we continually reject God's Word, we should not expect new guidance from Him. God has already spoken through His Word, and when we ignore it, our hearts grow hardened to His voice. That is the situation that Saul was in, and it was sad to see.

Look at 1 Samuel 28:12–15:

> When the woman saw Samuel, she cried out with a loud voice. And the woman spoke to Saul, saying, "Why have you deceived me? For you are Saul!" And the king said to her, "Do not be afraid. What did you see?" And the woman said to Saul, "I saw a spirit ascending out of the earth." So he said to her, "What is his form?" And she said, "An old man is coming up, and he is covered with a mantle." And Saul perceived that it was Samuel, and he stooped with his face to the ground and bowed down. Now Samuel said to Saul, "Why have you disturbed me by bringing me up?" And Saul answered, "I am deeply distressed; for the Philistines make war against me, and God has departed from me and does not answer me anymore, neither by prophets nor by dreams. Therefore I have called you, that you may reveal to me what I should do."

There is much debate about this whole episode, whether God allowed this and it was Samuel or perhaps a demonic impersonator. However, Samuel is named in the text as speaking. What is without debate is that Saul's rejection of God's Word made him a desperate man. His desperation did not bring him to his knees in repentance but, rather, to devices of the devil that ultimately lead to the grave. It reminds me of a proverb that Ben Franklin wrote in *Poor Richard's Almanack*: "For the want of a nail, the shoe was lost. For the want of a shoe, the horse was lost. For the want of a horse, the rider was lost. For the want of a rider, the battle was lost. For the want of a battle, the kingdom was lost."[3] For Saul, the battle, the kingdom, and his life were all lost, and it all traces back to his own pride and rejection of the Word of God.

How can we apply all of this? David refused to harm Saul even when it appeared that God had delivered his enemy into his hand because he knew that God's command mattered more than the circumstances before him. This reminds us that we must be careful not to interpret opportunities as permission to ignore God's Word. We also see David allowing fear to influence his thinking when he believed that Saul would eventually kill him, showing how easily fear can shape our decisions if we lose sight of God's promises. In contrast, Saul's continued rejection of God's Word eventually led him to seek guidance from forbidden sources rather than turning to the Lord. Ultimately, this passage reminds us that our help does not come from people or circumstances but from the Lord, the Maker of heaven and earth.

Prayer

Father, thank You for Your Word. Lord, we are grateful for the Holy Spirit, our teacher, leading us through this journey through Your Word. May You take the Word and help us to rightfully apply it to our lives. We pray, Lord, that we will not be like Saul, that we will not stop listening but, rather, that we will listen and obey, so that You will continue to speak to us and guide us through Your Word. May we never be in that desperate of a situation where we cannot hear You because we have not been listening. So, Father, make our hearts and our ears sensitive to the voice of the Holy Spirit as You speak to us through Your Word. We pray in Jesus's name. Amen.

Questions for Reflection and Discussion

1. Why did Saul and his men stay asleep when David and Abishai were walking in their camp (see 26:12)?
2. Why do you think Saul was so afraid when he saw the army of the Philistines (see 28:4–6)?

Notes on Today's Bible Reading

— Day 14 —

Today's Reading: 1 Samuel 29–31

Verse of the Day

> Then Saul said to his armorbearer, "Draw your sword, and thrust me through with it, lest these uncircumcised men come and thrust me through and abuse me." But his armorbearer would not, for he was greatly afraid. Therefore Saul took a sword and fell on it.
>
> *—1 Samuel 31:4*

Please read the entire Scripture selection in your own Bible and highlight or underline verses that stand out to you before you read the observations and engage the questions below.

Today, we are finishing the book of 1 Samuel and will delve into chapters 29–31. We see that the book begins on a much more positive note than it ends. A major takeaway from the book is the critical nature of leadership—parental, spiritual, and political. The health of a family, of the church, and of a nation stands or falls on the foundation of leadership. We see more of that message in these chapters.

Chapter 29 picks up with the Philistines preparing for war with Israel, as in chapter 28's opening verse. We begin in 1 Samuel 29:1–3:

> Then the Philistines gathered together all their armies at Aphek, and the Israelites encamped by a fountain which is in

> Jezreel. And the lords of the Philistines passed in review by hundreds and by thousands, but David and his men passed in review at the rear with Achish. Then the princes of the Philistines said, "What are these Hebrews doing here?" And Achish said to the princes of the Philistines, "Is this not David, the servant of Saul king of Israel, who has been with me these days, or these years? And to this day I have found no fault in him since he defected to me."

David had been in Ziklag, operating under the king of Gath's blessing. Recall that David was not being completely honest with him about his military operations. There are disputes about David's motives here. Some say he was ready to go to battle against Israel. Others say not. I believe he did not want to go to battle with Israel, given all that he had done previously to help the people of Israel who had been neglected by the leadership of Saul. We also know from multiple occasions that David was not going to lift his hand against Saul. Therefore, it is unlikely that he would fight Israel.

Unfortunately, we have limited information here, but it would be safe to assume that David was praying for a way out, and this was a part of his bad decision to go there to begin with. However, he was praying for God's guidance, and God directed him through His will. Sometimes, even when we make bad decisions, the Lord can work through them. This does not mean there are no consequences, as we will see. However, the Lord apparently provided a way out because there would be no way for him to be king if he had gone against the children of Israel in battle. So, the Philistine leader said, "No, David will not join us in battle against Israel." This was a major victory for David. He would not be going to battle against his own people and then be guilty of treason.

Next, Samuel 30 fits what might be referred to as the "Elijah effect," the spiritual backlash after a major victory. This was a major relief. He was not going to have to fight against Israel. Do you remember what happened with Elijah after God destroyed the prophets of Baal? Jezebel came after him, and he became so discouraged that he wanted to die.

We read about David's challenge in 1 Samuel 30:1–6a:

> Now it happened, when David and his men came to Ziklag, on the third day, that the Amalekites had invaded the South and Ziklag, attacked Ziklag and burned it with fire, and had taken captive the women and those who were there, from small to great; they did not kill anyone, but carried them away and went their way. So David and his men came to the city, and there it was, burned with fire; and their wives, their sons, and their daughters had been taken captive. Then David and the people who were with him lifted up their voices and wept, until they had no more power to weep. And David's two wives, Ahinoam the Jezreelitess, and Abigail the widow of Nabal the Carmelite, had been taken captive. Now David was greatly distressed, for the people spoke of stoning him, because the soul of all the people was grieved, every man for his sons and his daughters.

It is difficult to imagine anything worse for David than this situation. Remember, these six hundred men who were with David had been in debt, discontent, and distress. Things quickly spun out of control. This was a true test of David's leadership. He was personally distraught. He had lost his wives and all that he had, and he was leading men who had major issues. Therefore, they were not in a good place to begin with, but when they lost everything, they held David responsible as their leader. David did three important things that are critical in a crisis and are a model for us.

We read about these in 1 Samuel 30:6b–9: "But David strengthened himself in the Lord his God. Then David said to Abiathar the priest, Ahimelech's son, 'Please bring the ephod here to me.' And

Abiathar brought the ephod to David. So David inquired of the Lord, saying, 'Shall I pursue this troop? Shall I overtake them?' And He answered him, 'Pursue, for you shall surely overtake them and without fail recover all.' So David went, he and the six hundred men who were with him, and came to the Brook Besor, where those stayed who were left behind."

First, we see at the end of verse 6 that David strengthened and encouraged himself in the Lord. What did he do specifically? Based upon what we do know about David from Scripture, it is probable that he worshipped the Lord. David was a worshipper. He recounted God's faithfulness. I think this is one of the things we need to do when we are in a difficult situation. A grateful heart, even in the midst of a difficult season, can find peace and comfort in knowing that God is, always has been, and always will be faithful. That is the first thing David did: worship. Furthermore, we see this sentiment at the end of his life. Psalm 37:25, "I have been young, and now am old; yet I have not seen the righteous forsaken, nor his descendants begging bread." God is faithful, and we need to thank God even during difficult seasons. David strengthened himself in the Lord.

Second, David inquired of the Lord; he prayed. Too often, in crisis situations, believers turn to everyone but God. He did not form a committee for a discussion. He did not put it out on Facebook for advice. He simply got on his face before the Lord. He prayed. David inquired of the Lord.

Third, David took action. First he worshipped, then he prayed, but ultimately he put his faith and his prayers into action with a plan that would shift the men's focus from their dire circumstances into a solution. That is vitally important.

So, what was the result? Look at 1 Samuel 30:18–19: "So David recovered all that the Amalekites had carried away, and David rescued his two wives. And nothing of theirs was lacking, either small or great, sons or daughters, spoil or anything which they had taken from them; David recovered all." We have yet another example of David's challenges with the men he was leading and the wisdom he had to lead them. This was a time of testing and preparation for David. Oftentimes, when things do not unfold the way we want, and we walk through difficult circumstances and challenges, it is all preparation. It is preparation for God's plan and purpose.

Let us continue in 1 Samuel 30:22: "Then all the wicked and worthless men of those who went with David answered and said, 'Because they did not go with us, we will not give them any of the spoil that we have recovered, except for every man's wife and children, that they may lead them away and depart.'" So, what happened? At the brook of Bezar, two hundred stayed behind. They were just too tired; they could not go any further. Four hundred went on. And eventually, when the four hundred came back, they had not only what had been theirs; they had more, and they did not want to give the two hundred anything.

Note how David responded in 1 Samuel 30:23–24: "But David said, 'My brethren, you shall not do so with what the Lord has given us, who has preserved us and delivered into our hand the troop that came against us. For who will heed you in this matter? But as his part is who goes down to the battle, so shall his part be who stays by the supplies; they shall share alike.'" David understood the vital role each person played, whether on the front lines or in a supporting role. That is a very important leadership principle we can glean from this passage. Then we see David's political acumen, his insight, and understanding: "Now when David came to Ziklag, he sent some of the spoil to the elders of Judah, to his friends, saying, 'Here is a present for you from the spoil of the enemies of the Lord'" (v. 26).

In this chapter, we see God at work. While David placed himself in a difficult situation among the Philistines, God providentially used the concerns of the Philistine leaders to remove him from a battle against Israel. This is a reminder that the Lord can redirect our path even when we make poor decisions. When David returned to Ziklag and found that everything had been taken, he strengthened himself in the Lord and inquired of the Lord before acting, demonstrating to us the importance of turning to God for strength in times of crisis. David then sought the Lord's guidance before pursuing the enemy, showing that wisdom begins with seeking God's will and direction. Finally, when the victory was won, David ensured that both the men who fought and those who stayed behind shared in the reward. This is a great reminder that every role matters in the work God is accomplishing.

In chapter 31, we see how the men of Jabesh Gilead provided the bookends to Saul's reign as king. Jabesh Gilead was the city that the Ammonites said, "We will make peace with you. We will enter into a treaty if you will serve us. But you have to let us put out your right eyes." Remember, they asked for help, and Saul responded. This was his first test as the newly anointed king. The Spirit of God came upon Saul. He responded, and that successful military campaign solidified his leadership. However, we read in this final chapter of the tragic death of Saul and his sons and the defeat of Israel at the hands of the Philistines, who proceeded to desecrate the dead body of the king. They cut off his head, stripped his armor and placed it in the temple of Ashtaroth, and fastened his body to the wall of Beth Shan (see 31:9–10).

Drop down to 1 Samuel 31:11–12: "Now when the inhabitants of Jabesh Gilead heard what the Philistines had done to Saul, all the valiant men arose and traveled all night, and took the body of Saul and the bodies of his sons from the wall of Beth Shan; and they came to Jabesh and burned them there." One must appreciate what these "valiant men" did because they were expressing appreciation and gratitude for what Saul had done for their city, even though he had gone off the rails later. Saul's life was a tragic example of what happens when we reject the Word of God. It had consequences that impacted not only him and his family but the entire nation. The same is true for each one of us.

Another important detail in chapter 31 is the way Saul's life ended. After being wounded in battle and seeing that defeat was certain, Saul said to his armorbearer, "'Draw your sword, and thrust me through with it,'" but when the armorbearer refused, "Saul took a sword and fell on it" (1 Sam. 31:4). This is a sobering conclusion to the life of Israel's first king. Saul began with great promise, yet his story reminds us that a strong beginning does not guarantee a faithful finish. Over time, his repeated rejection of the Word of the Lord hardened his heart and led him further away from God. Even so, God's purposes were not thwarted. While Saul's reign came to an end, the Lord was already preparing David to lead Israel. This passage reminds us of the importance of remaining faithful to God's Word throughout our lives so that we may finish well. We end this book with the people both mourning a king and still longing for a king. God is preparing such a king in David, a man after God's own heart.

Prayer

Father, thank You for Your Word. Once again, Lord, we are grateful for the insight and understanding. And Lord, as we complete this first book of Samuel, we just continue to ask the Holy Spirit to guide us. May we take the principles of Your Word and apply them to our lives that we might honor You in all that we do. In Jesus's name. Amen.

Questions for Reflection and Discussion

1. Achish dismissed David because the Philistine kings were afraid he might join Saul and turn against them, but why do you think God may have used their concern to remove David from this battle (see 29:1–7)?

2. In the wake of the attack on Ziklag and David's men turning on him in distress, how did David find the strength to continue (see 30:6–9)?

Notes on Today's Bible Reading

Conclusion

As we come to the end of our study of 1 Samuel, we are left with a question that reaches far beyond these stories of ancient Israel and into the very core of our lives: Who will be our king? This was a defining issue for Israel, and it remains the defining issue for us today. The people of Israel believed that a human king would provide the security, identity, and direction they longed for. Yet their experience revealed that no earthly leader could meet the deepest needs of the human heart.

The king they chose in Saul had all the appearances of being everything they wanted. He was physically commanding, capable, and impressive in the eyes of others. However, his life ultimately demonstrated that outward success cannot replace inward obedience. His failure was not primarily in his physical attributes and abilities but in his heart. He rejected God's word, and God rejected him as king.

David, on the other hand, was chosen not because of outward qualifications but because of his heart. Though he was flawed and made serious mistakes, his life was marked by prayerful humility and a genuine dependence on the Lord. David's story reminds us that God is not seeking perfection but a heart that passionately pursues Him.

Ultimately, the story of 1 Samuel points us beyond both Saul and David to a greater King. Israel's longing for a king was fulfilled in a way they could not have fully understood at the time. From the line of David came Jesus Christ, the perfect and eternal King. Where Saul failed, Jesus obeyed completely. Where David stumbled, Jesus remained without sin. Where earthly kingdoms rise and fall, His reign stands forever.

The question, then, is not whether God has provided the King—He has. The question is whether we will submit to Him. In our own lives, we may not express it in the same way Israel did, but we are often tempted to place our trust in things we can see and control. For stability and direction, we look to our own abilities, our plans, or the systems around us. Yet none of these can carry us through difficulty or defeat the enemy of our souls. Only Christ can truly lead, sustain, and deliver.

As we conclude this study, take time to reflect honestly before the Lord. Consider where your trust truly lies and whether your heart is fully surrendered to Him. The call of 1 Samuel is not simply to learn from the past, but to respond to God in the present. God is still seeking those whose hearts are fully devoted to Him. May your life be marked not by outward appearance but by inward faithfulness.

Prayer

Father, we thank You for this insightful book of 1 Samuel where we read of the people longing for a king. Yet Lord they had everything they needed in You. May we understand the same. You have provided us with King Jesus, the greater Son of David. May He reign over every part of our lives. May our hearts passionately pursue Him, His righteousness, and His kingdom, for Your glory. In Jesus's name we pray. Amen.

Appendix 1:
Stand on the Word Bible Reading Plan

Visit frc.org/Bible for our chronological journey through the Bible that we call "Stand on the Word." We encourage you to spend time reading and studying the Bible because it is literally "God-breathed" (2 Tim. 3:16 NIV); it is God's very words to us. The Bible answers the big questions, such as, Why am I here? Where did I come from? Where am I going (life after death)? If God is good, why does evil and suffering exist? The Bible not only answers these big questions; it offers practical advice in areas such as, How can I deal with feelings of fear or anger or guilt? How can I forgive when I cannot forget? What should I look for in a spouse? How can I have a successful marriage? How can I be a good parent? What is my spiritual gift and place in the church? What is my stewardship responsibility as a citizen? We learned the verse in Bible school, "Your word is a lamp to my feet and a light to my path" (Ps. 119:105). God's Word shows us the way forward in any area of life and on every question we face.

The Stand on the Word Bible Reading Plan takes us through the Bible chronologically. In other words, each reading takes us through the Bible as events occurred in history as far as it is possible. Here is how it works for our family. At the same time each morning, whether I am at home, in Washington, or some foreign country, I send my wife and children a morning greeting along with a reminder of the passage for the day. The text includes two questions related to the reading. The questions are designed to help in content retention, serve as an accountability tool, and provide for discussion.

The two-year plan does not have a Sunday passage. Instead, it provides an outline for a family discussion that can be done on Sunday afternoon or evening. Our family has incorporated the discussion into our Sunday lunch, which follows a biblical model of life enriching conversations over a meal. The weekly discussion time begins with a spiritual leader asking each person individually for one or two insights or truths they gained from their reading during the week and how those truths apply to our lives. After everyone else shares, the father or group leader can lead a short discussion of one of the passages that was read during the week and how it applies to our lives here and now. It is also a time for them to ask questions.

By the way, you don't have to have all the answers. If you don't know, tell them so, then talk to your pastor or other trusted person with Bible knowledge. If your children start asking questions, that suggests they are thinking about what they are reading.

Reading God's Word will help you establish a fruitful walk with the God who made you and loves you. Whether you are single or married, this plan will enable you to lead your friends and family in daily reading God's Word. The added benefit is that you will all be reading the same text together. It will amaze you to see how God speaks sometimes in the same ways and at other times in different ways to each of you. Being on this journey together will build a spiritual synergy, a deep bond, and sense of unity and purpose like nothing else! Use it to impart the Word of life. Visit frc.org/Bible to sign up or simply download the Stand Firm App.

Appendix 2:
Prayer: Talking with God

Most Americans say they pray, but not as many pray the way Jesus did and taught His disciples to pray. Fewer, still, really know the power in prayer that God gave us to impact our families, communities, nation, and world. But prayer is our lifeline to God, our means of communicating with our heavenly Father. It develops our relationship—our friendship, fellowship, and intimacy—with Him. In prayer we experience God and are "filled with the Spirit" (Eph. 5:18–21). God uses the prayers of faithful men, women, boys, and girls to heal broken lives and strengthen families, churches, communities, and even nations. He uses our prayers to advance His kingdom on earth (Daniel 9; Acts 4:36)! He wants to so use all believers!

The Essence of Prayer

Prayer is simply talking with God—about anything and everything. He is our Maker, Father, Savior, Provider, and Counselor, our Master, Healer, Guide, and Friend. Christ died for our sins and rose from the dead to sit at the right hand of God the Father, where He is praying for us right now (Heb. 10:12). His Spirit now lives within us and helps us to pray (1 John 4:16).

The Priority of Prayer

Jesus spent time alone with God regularly drawing strength from the Father and seeking His will for every decision (Luke 6:12–13;

22:39–44). His disciples asked Jesus to teach them how to pray (Luke 11:1–13). The apostles knew that prayer and obedience were the keys to Christ's life and ministry and were determined to follow His example: "[W]e will devote ourselves to prayer and to the ministry of the word" (Acts 6:4 ESV). Too few American men pray today, even pastors and leaders! Yet strong praying men are the norm in Scripture. Our families, churches, and nation need men who will make prayer a priority today! (1 Tim. 2:8)

The Practice of Prayer

Scripture teaches, "Pray continually!" (1 Thess. 5:17 NIV); "Praying always" (Eph. 6:18); "Always pray and not give up" (Luke 18:1 NIV). Below are some helps to get you started. No one can beat the Lord's Prayer. It is an outline of key themes to guide our prayer lives:

> "Our Father in heaven,
> hallowed be your name.
> Your kingdom come,
> your will be done,
>   on earth as it is in heaven.
> Give us this day our daily bread,
> and forgive us our debts,
>   as we also have forgiven our debtors.
> And lead us not into temptation,
>   but deliver us from evil." (Matt. 6:9–13 ESV)

In the book of Psalms and throughout Scripture, God has sprinkled prayers: patterns for us to learn from. Here is a simple, popular acronym to help jog our memories:

P-R-A-Y:

- ***Praise:*** Our Father in heaven, hallowed be your name.
- ***Repent:*** And forgive us our debts, as we also have forgiven our debtors.
- ***Ask:*** Give us this day our daily bread, and forgive us our debts, as we also have forgiven our debtors. And lead us not into temptation, but deliver us from evil.
- ***Yield:*** Your kingdom come, your will be done, on earth as it is in heaven.

Praying Through Scripture

God also talks to us. The Bible is His Word (2 Tim. 2:15; 3:16). Bible in hand, we should pray God's promises back to Him, and claim them for our families, our work, our finances, and our nation (1 Tim. 2:1–8; 1 John 5:14–15).

Scriptures to Pray as a Man: Joshua 1:8; 1 Timothy 3:1–15; 1 Chronicles 12:32; 1 Timothy 6:1–12; 1 Corinthians 16:13; Romans 12:1–21; Micah 6:8; John 4:24; Acts 2:38; 1 Kings 2:2; Husbands: Ephesians 5:25–28; Genesis 2:24; 1 Peter 3:7; Ephesians 4:26–27; Matthew 5:32; Proverbs 5:19; 1 Corinthians 6:18; Fathers: Deuteronomy 4:8–10; 11:18–21; Exodus 34:5–8; Psalm 127:3–5; Matthew 7:11; Ephesians 6:4; Proverbs 22:6; Luke 11:11–12; Hebrews 12:5–7

Scriptures to Pray as a Woman: Matthew 22:36–40; Proverbs 31:30; 1 Peter 3:1–3; Ephesians 5:26; Ephesians 4:15, 29; 1 Timothy 3:11; Ephesians 5:22, 24; 1 Peter 3:1–2; Philippians 4:10–13; Philippians 2:3–4; Proverbs 31:12; 1 Corinthians 7:34; Titus 2:3–4; Titus 2:4–5; James 1:19; Ephesians 4:32; 1 Corinthians 7:1–5; Luke 2:37; Colossians 4:2; Proverbs 31:27; 1 Timothy 5:14

Scriptures to Pray for Your Children: Matthew 22:36–40; 2 Timothy 3:15; Psalm 97:10, 38:18; Proverbs 8:13; John 17:15, 10:10;

Romans 12:9; Psalm 119:71; Hebrews 12:5–6; Daniel 1:17, 20; Proverbs 1:4; James 1:5; Romans 13:1; Ephesians 6:1–3; Hebrews 13:17; Proverbs 1:10–16, 13:20; 2 Corinthians 6:14–17; Deuteronomy 6; 1 Corinthians 6:18–20; Acts 24:16; 1 Timothy 1:19, 4:1–2; Titus 1:15–16; Psalm 23:4; Deuteronomy 10:12; Matthew 28:18–20; Ephesians 1:3, 4:29; Ephesians 1:16–19; Philippians 1:11; Colossians 1:9; Philippians 1:9–10

Developing Personal Prayer Habits

Rise early each day to pray with opened Bible. Daniel prayed three times daily. Pray whenever you can: as you drive, with your wife, with your children at dinner and before bedtime. You cannot pray too much!

Praying Together with Others

Pray with your spouse regularly. Make time for family prayer. Be part of your church prayer meeting or group. Christ said, "My house shall be called a house of prayer." The apostle Paul instructed Pastor Timothy (1 Tim. 2:1–8) to make prayer the first order of the church, saying prayer is key to peace in the nation. There is nothing like a Spirit-led prayer meeting with people who love the Lord! Praying women have been standing in the prayer gap for decades. Every man must set his heart to become a praying man, lead his family in prayer, and be a strong contributor to the corporate prayer life of his church. We must be leaders in praying for our morally and spiritually troubled, divided nation—and for our national leaders. American Christians simply must respond to God's promise: "If My people who are called by My name will humble themselves, and pray and seek My face, and turn from their wicked ways, then I will hear from heaven, and will forgive their sin and heal their land" (2 Chron. 7:14).

Prayer As Warfare

Jesus described the enemy, the devil, as a thief whose mission is "to steal, and to kill, and to destroy" (John 10:10). Demonic forces are at war against everything good in you, your family, your church, your community, America, and every nation (Eph. 6:10–20).

The devil and his minions are out to thwart the kingdom of God and eliminate righteousness wherever he can. He hates God, hates people, and will use spiritually ignorant and deceived men, women, boys, and girls to do his bidding. Men of God today, like the sons of Issachar in ancient Israel, need to understand the times and know what the church and our nation must do (1 Chron. 12:32). We must pull down Satan's strongholds, wrestle for our families, and use Spirit-led prayer and wisdom to help guide our churches and communities to prevail against the evil onslaught against us (2 Cor. 10:3–5). This is the war of the ages and it is real.

Finally, Determine to Become a Person of Prayer

No matter how long you have been a Christian and may have neglected prayer up until now, you can become a person of prayer starting today. If you have missed the mark, it is not too late. Call upon the Lord, ask His help, and proceed with His guidance. *O Lord, make me a praying person; make me a prayer warrior! In Jesus's name, amen!*

Appendix 3:
How to Share Your Faith

Recent polling from Lifeway Research shows that "only 3 in 10 unchurched Americans (29%) say a Christian has ever shared with them one-on-one how a person becomes a Christian."[4]

Even less are successful in helping someone make a decision to follow Christ. Maybe that is why this whole notion of sharing your faith is so intimidating for many. However, it does not have to be. The best place to start is with your story. Some call it a testimony. In a courtroom, testimony is relied on as part of the evidence in a case. As you are telling your story, you are presenting evidence for how Christ has changed your life for the better. If you are speaking with another man about your faith, think in terms of telling your story in three parts:

1. Your life before you became a follower of Christ.
2. Your encounter with Christ and your decision to follow him as your Savior and Lord.
3. Your life since becoming as a follower of Christ.

The great apostle Paul told his faith story numerous times—several of them are recorded in the Bible. You'll notice these same three parts in Acts 22.

1. Life Before Christ

First of all, notice what Paul said about his life before Christ:

"I am a Jew, born in Tarsus in Cilicia, but brought up in this city, educated at the feet of Gamaliel according to the strict

> manner of the law of our fathers, being zealous for God as all of you are this day. I persecuted this Way to the death, binding and delivering to prison both men and women, as the high priest and the whole council of elders can bear me witness. From them I received letters to the brothers, and I journeyed toward Damascus to take those also who were there and bring them in bonds to Jerusalem to be punished." (Acts 22:3–5 ESV)

If there was ever a Jew who was steeped in religion, that Jew was Paul. His religious trophy case was filled to overflowing (v. 3). Over in Philippians 3, he pulled out and dusted off several of them. Then he described his radical commitment to his religion to the point of persecuting followers of Christ (vv. 4–5). Take time to write out what you remember about your life before your life-changing encounter with Christ. Be brief and to the point:

2. Encounter with Christ

Paul not only told about his life before Christ, but then he shared his life-changing encounter with Christ:

> "As I was on my way and drew near to Damascus, about noon a great light from heaven suddenly shone around me. And I fell to the ground and heard a voice saying to me, 'Saul, Saul, why are you persecuting me?' And I answered, 'Who are you, Lord?' And he said to me, 'I am Jesus of Nazareth, whom you are persecuting.' Now those who were with me saw the light but did not understand the voice of the one who was speaking to me." (Acts 22:6–9 ESV)

Notice Paul said in verse 9: "Who are you, Lord?" He was told by a heavenly voice: "I am Jesus of Nazareth, whom you are persecuting." What an amazing encounter! Obviously, most people don't get blinded by a light or hear voices from heaven. However, your story of your encounter with Christ is unique, and no doubt it was (and hopefully still is) a powerful experience for you. Take time to write out your encounter with Christ and how you came to make the decision to follow him as Savior and Lord, but don't rush it. Tell what happened in detail:

3. Life-Change After Christ

Paul then began to tell about the changes in his life after his encounter with Christ:

> "And I said, 'What shall I do, Lord?' And the Lord said to me, 'Rise, and go into Damascus, and there you will be told all that is appointed for you to do.' And since I could not see because of the brightness of that light, I was led by the hand by those who were with me, and came into Damascus.
>
> "And one Ananias, a devout man according to the law, well spoken of by all the Jews who lived there, came to me, and standing by me said to me, 'Brother Saul, receive your sight.' And at that very hour I received my sight and saw him. And he said, 'The God of our fathers appointed you to know his will, to see the Righteous One and to hear a voice from his mouth; for you will be a witness for him to everyone of what you have seen and heard. And now why do you wait? Rise and be baptized and wash away your sins, calling on his name.'" (Acts 22:10–16 ESV)

In verse 10, Paul asked, basically, "Lord, what next?" and the risen Christ told him, "You will be told all that is appointed for you to do." And then Ananias, another disciple of Jesus, communicated Paul's assignment in verses 13–16, which was basically to give his testimony and tell his story "to all people." Obviously, Paul accepted his assignment and went on to become one of the greatest leaders in the history of the Christian faith, going on missionary journeys, leading multitudes to faith in Jesus, planting churches, ordaining leaders, even giving his testimony to officials in Rome, which was the capital of the ancient world. He also experienced persecution, imprisonment, and finally death for his faith. Again, Paul's story can be intimidating, but it doesn't need to be. Just think about how your life has changed since you began following Christ. Write down some of your thoughts. Remember, you are trying to offer compelling evidence.

Having read how Paul told his faith story, use the outline above and write out yours. Once you have written it, read through it and prayerfully edit it. After you feel good about it, practice sharing it with another trusted and seasoned believer, preferably someone who has successfully helped lead someone else to faith in Christ. Then you may want to go back and edit it again as you may have thought about a better way to communicate it. Finally, pray for God to open a door of opportunity to share your faith story with someone. Pray that the Holy Spirit will prepare the way for you and do only what He can do. At the end of our best efforts to share Christ, it is still up to God and the individual.

Appendix 4:
The Solution to Our Greatest Challenge

What is the greatest challenge facing families and the church today? It is a lack of a biblical worldview. A worldview is the lens through which we view life and the world around us. Having a biblical worldview means the Bible is our lens. Everything in life is filtered through and viewed from a biblical perspective. The problem is that very few can truthfully claim that the Bible is their authoritative point of reference for what they value and how they behave. In fact, renowned researcher Dr. George Barna has found through extensive surveys measuring against seven core principles foundational to a biblical worldview that only 4 percent of Americans actually view their world through a biblical lens.[5]

What complicates matters is that our worldview is largely developed during childhood. Dr. Barna, Senior Research Fellow for the Center for Biblical Worldview at Family Research Council, has determined that a person's worldview is primarily established between the ages of fifteen months and thirteen years.[6] The problem is that the vast majority of kids reach their teenage years without a biblical worldview.

Here is more definitive evidence. The Nehemiah Institute, founded in 1986, is on a mission to provide worldview assessment to youth in Christian homes associated with Christian schools, homeschool associations, and church youth groups.[7] Called "PEERS," it is the only professionally validated worldview assessment available that I'm aware of. It's fairly comprehensive with seventy test items, fourteen in each category, that the kids take, and it breaks down the results. All the students who take the test fall into four broad categories of worldview:

- Biblical Theism (meaning a Biblical Worldview)
- Moderate Christian
- Secular Humanism
- Socialism

Keep in mind that this is only self-described Christian kids in Christian schools, youth groups, or homeschool. Based on almost forty years of results, PEERS testing shows that a majority of youth from Christian homes are abandoning a biblical worldview and biblical theism in favor of a secular worldview, if not a socialist worldview. When PEERS was first launched in the 1980s, the majority of youth from Christian homes scored mainly in either the moderate Christian worldview or biblical theism worldview. Today, the same demographic shows more than 90 percent of Christian youth scoring in the secular humanism category using the exact same questions that were used in the 1980s, and less than 3 percent are scoring in the biblical theism category. Again, these are kids in Christian schools, church youth groups, and homeschool.

Consequently, this is arguably the single greatest problem facing families and the church in America today, and why we must teach our children. We should not be surprised by these numbers when we are outsourcing the education of our children to people who, for the most part, not only don't have a biblical worldview, but many have an antibiblical worldview. This is why Scripture tells parents that we are primarily responsible to talk about God's Word with our children "when you sit in your house, when you walk by the way, when you lie down, and when you rise up" (see Deut. 6:4–9). We should be teaching our children and our grandchildren the Word of God and its application to our world. Yet when we outsource that to someone else, we see sad results. Of course, we must factor in that it is not simply what's happening in a classroom; it is also shaped by what they're listening to, watching, and engaging with on social media, etc. Furthermore, parents cannot give what they don't have. So, if parents don't have a biblical worldview, they cannot give their children a biblical worldview. And you cannot get a biblical worldview unless you are regularly reading the Word of God.

That brings me to the proposed solution. Again, to gain a biblical worldview, a person must be regularly reading and studying and applying the Word of God. That is what spurred me to develop our Stand on the Word Bible Reading Plan. It is a two-year, chronologically prioritized Bible reading plan that takes ten to fifteen minutes a day of reading, six days a week, Monday through Saturday. On Sunday, there's no reading because it's a discussion day for the family, a day to reflect on what we have read over the previous week and share how God is speaking to us.

This Bible reading plan came about a number of years ago when I was looking for a devotional book for our family—something that would allow five children, ranging from two to eighteen years old, to have a conversation. A lot of people send me books and devotionals with an interest in being a guest on *Washington Watch* to talk about their book, so I had a good handle on pretty much everything that was out there. I looked for six months—read them, studied them, went through them myself—and couldn't find anything that I felt would work. Finally, the Holy Spirit said, "Try the Bible."

So, we began with a couple of books from the New Testament, letters of Paul, and then I began to look at how we could take the entire Bible, breaking it up into a two-year reading plan as opposed to a one-year plan. The latter, for most people, becomes like a speed reading course where not much gets absorbed. However, with the two-year plan, everyone can read it in bite-sized chunks, and each day comes with two questions for reflection. The questions also served as an accountability to gauge who in the family was reading the chapters. And wherever I might be in the world, I would set my clock so that at 7 a.m. central time I would text my family the reading for the day and the two associated questions.

Then on Sunday, after lunch, we would have a conversation about the chapters we read that week and how it applies to the world in which we live. Our weekly time together as a family became the highlight of my week. Here is a suggested template for your gathering:

- Opening Prayer – Praise and a brief prayer for spiritual insight and unity.
- Recap – Briefly summarize the chapters covered that week.
- Discussion Questions – Use open-ended, age-appropriate prompts to spark meaningful worldview conversations. Here are some suggestions:
    1. Most meaningful passage that spoke to you personally?
    2. Insights gained about God: Who He is, What He values and expects, How He works?
    3. Applications that we can make from the Word to what is happening in the world?
    4. How would God have you apply His truth to your life personally?
- Action Steps – Encourage each family member to share a personal takeaway or action step for living the truth revealed in God's Word.
- Closing Prayer – Conclude by praising God for how He has revealed Himself, His purposes, and His ways, and by praying for His help in living in the light of His truth and sharing it with others during the week ahead.

For our family, these Sunday gatherings were nearly as meaningful as a church worship service! Now that nearly all of our kids are grown and some are establishing their own families, I pray they will do the same with their children as God gives them. But that was the strategy we used, and God has blessed it.

That Sunday debrief time is a key part of this strategy to develop a biblical worldview. The inspiration for it came about from a trip I took a number of years ago to Israel and attended a Shabbat dinner with a family. I was fascinated with the conversation around the dinner table, talking about the application of God's Word to the world in which we live. And I thought, "You know, that is what's missing, a conversation to help develop a biblical worldview." I had one child who was in college at the time. So, on Sunday we would dissect what they were being taught (because it was a secular college) and equip them to counter those arguments that they were hearing. We were honing her biblical worldview.

The bottom line here is that it is vitally important that we are intentional about cultivating a biblical worldview in our family members as well as with church members. I believe that reading the Bible daily, with a daily touch-of-base about the reading, followed by an extended weekend conversation can provide the solution to the challenge of making sure our families and our churches develop a biblical worldview. I pray you will join us on this Stand on the Word journey through the Bible. Visit frc.org/Bible to sign up or simply download the Stand Firm app.

Notes

1. Josephus, *Antiquities of the Jews*, 5.10.4, https://www.gutenberg.org.

2. See Karoline Leonard, "Scroll call: Study finds Americans checked their phones nearly 200 times a day in 2025," *Austin American-Statesman*, December 30, 2025, https://www.statesman.com/business/technology/article/screentime-americans-phone-checks-5–min-21266440.php.

3.Benjamin Franklin, *Poor Richard's Almanack* (Waterloo, IA: U.S.C. Publishing CO., 1914), 22.

4. https://research.lifeway.com/2021/09/09/christians-dont-share-faith-with-unchurched-friends/

5. Tracy Munsil, "Barna, CRC: Widespread Worldview Confusion Grows as Americans Redefine God," Arizona Christian University, February 18, 2025, https://www.arizonachristian.edu/2025/02/18/awvi-2025_01_most-americans-believe-in-a-supreme-power-but-not-the-god-of-the-bible/.

6. Tracy Munsil, "Most US Kids Ages 8-12 Lack Biblical 'Cornerstones,' Research Says," Arizona Christian University, October 11, 2023, https://www.arizonachristian.edu/2023/10/11/most-us-kids-ages-8-12-lack-biblical-cornerstones/.

7. https://www.worldviewcheckup.org/.

Other **STAND on the WORD** Study Guides Available from Fidelis Publishing and Family Research Council

Genesis: Book of Beginnings ISBN: 9798993655079
Joshua: Finish Strong! ISBN: 9781956454802
Nehemiah: Rebuilding a Nation ISBN: 9781956454468
Jeremiah: Courage in a Cancel Culture ISBN: 9781956454369
Daniel: Visions and Valor ISBN: 9798992418651
Matthew: The King and His Kingdom ISBN: 9798992418682
Ephesians: Keep Standing! ISBN: 9781956454659
Paul's Prison Letters ISBN: 9798999024657
Paul's Letters to Leaders ISBN: 9798999024664

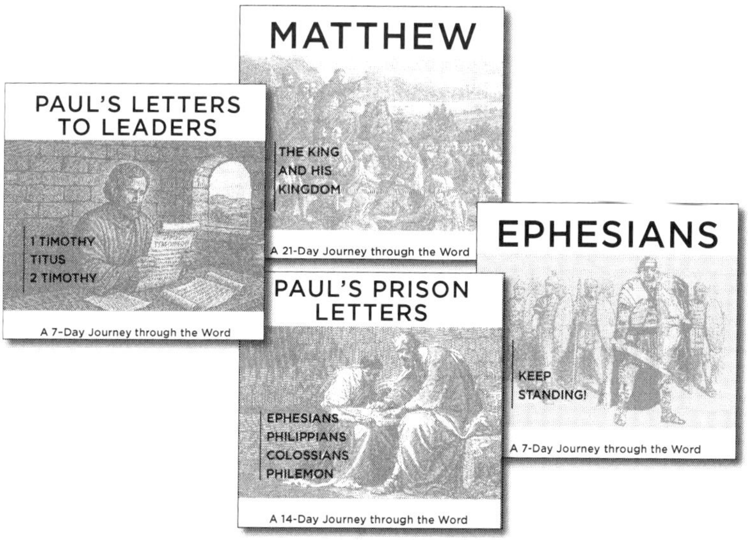

Also from Fidelis Publishing and Family Research Council

STAND on the WORD Journals

Volume 1
ISBN: 9781956454758

Volume 2
ISBN: 9781956454871